THE HOUSE OF
VIKTOR & ROLF

Caroline Evans and Susannah Frankel

Edited by Jane Alison and Ariella Yedgar

MERRELL
LONDON · NEW YORK

CONTENTS

PREFACE

When we invited Viktor & Rolf to create a retrospective exhibition of their last fifteen years' work in fashion, they approached the challenge with the creativity and criticality that characterize everything they do. Most fashion exhibitions follow a set formula: they tend to be structured chronologically, with precious pieces from key collections presented on mannequins, usually encased inside glass vitrines. At the Barbican, Viktor & Rolf have embraced this exhibition form while subtly re-imagining it. They have created an exhibition in which the viewer is at once physically excluded from, and then dramatically included in, the space of their works.

Similarly, Viktor & Rolf have, throughout their career, subverted not just the format of the catwalk show but also the time and space of fashion itself, thereby unsettling the viewer's normal experience of it. Their most radical reworking of a fashion presentation was probably the 'Russian Doll' collection (Autumn/Winter 1999–2000) – actually a Russian doll in reverse – conceived not sequentially as one thing after another but sculpturally as one thing placed on top of the previous. In the 'Atomic Bomb' (Autumn/Winter 1998–99) and 'Black Light' (Spring/Summer 1999) collections, each garment existed not in a single immutable state but in a state of before and after. The 'Upside Down' collection (Spring/Summer 2006), which consisted of inverted gowns, was staged in reverse, finale first. In the 'Black Hole' collection (Autumn/Winter 2001–02), black-painted models were visually flattened to become two-dimensional silhouettes rather than three-dimensional beings.

The House of Viktor & Rolf is both a building within a building and a fashion retrospective. Perfectly tailored to the brutalist spaces of the Barbican Art Gallery, with its double-height area and multi-roomed mezzanine, Viktor & Rolf's giant doll's house accommodates miniature mannequins that are, at the same time, oversized Victorian dolls, dressed in meticulously crafted, precisely scaled-down garments. Upstairs, in the eight bays comprising the upper gallery, it is as if the dolls have been suddenly scaled up to human size, giving visitors the uncanny feeling that they have entered the rooms of the doll's house. It is a delightful, Alice-in-Wonderland conceit, playful yet darkly surreal at the same time.

For Viktor & Rolf, couture is an artistic medium, a commodity, and a laboratory of ideas. They are fashion designers who make iconic, exquisite, technically breathtaking clothes. They are celebrants of their craft and yet, at the same time, trenchant commentators on the aspirational industry within which they work and within which they too aspire. Like Andy Warhol and Jeff Koons, Viktor & Rolf understand that great art is not simply about creating great and original works, but is in itself a philosophical exploration of the limits and possibilities of the medium in the context of the wider culture.

We are honoured that Viktor & Rolf have chosen to present their first British solo exhibition at the Barbican Art Gallery, and we are thrilled to be able to bring the work of these exceptional artists to the attention of a broad public audience, both in the United Kingdom and abroad.

We are indebted to the following for their generous loans to the exhibition: Centraal Museum, Utrecht, The Netherlands; Galliera, Musée de la Mode de la Ville de Paris, France; Groninger Museum, Groningen, The Netherlands; Han Nefkens, H+F Collection; The Kyoto Costume Institute, Japan; Her Royal Highness Princess Mabel van Oranje-Nassau; Rob van de Ven and Corinne Groot, Amsterdam; Witzenhausen Gallery, Amsterdam; Zuiderzee Museum, Enkhuizen, The Netherlands.

This sumptuous book to accompany the exhibition contains the work of many esteemed fashion photographers too numerous to mention. We are especially grateful, however, to Peter Stigter, Inez van Lamsweerde and Vinoodh Matadin, Anuschka Blommers and Niels Schumm, and Wendelien Daan, each of whom has worked closely with Viktor & Rolf over many years, for giving us the permission to use so many of their images.

We are deeply grateful to Viktor & Rolf and their team for the great vision and commitment they have brought to this ambitious project; Siebe Tettero, for the breathtaking design of the exhibition; FUEL, for the smart and imaginative design of this book and the exhibition graphics; and all at Merrell Publishers and at Karla Otto, Viktor & Rolf's PR agency.

The House of Viktor & Rolf would not have been possible without the support of the many organizations and public institutions that recognized the worth of this project and assisted in making it a reality. Premsela, Dutch Platform for Design and Fashion, has provided invaluable help towards the origination of the installation and has been a collaborating partner in our events programme. We are indebted to the VandenEnde Foundation for generously and enthusiastically supporting the exhibition at a critical moment in its genesis. The substantial contribution of the Mondriaan Foundation, Amsterdam, has been equally valuable.

We are very grateful to KLM Royal Dutch Airlines, who have supported the project generously. The Embassy of the Kingdom of The Netherlands and the Netherlands Board of Tourism & Conventions have been wonderfully supportive throughout. Finally, we have been fortunate enough to have *Elle* magazine as our media sponsors; they have been a delight to work with.

Graham Sheffield
Artistic Director

Kate Bush
Head of Art Galleries
Barbican Centre

INTRODUCTION

CAROLINE EVANS

Viktor Horsting and Rolf Snoeren graduated in 1992 from the fashion department of the Arnhem Academy of Art and Design in The Netherlands. They immediately moved to Paris and began to produce their own fashion designs in their free time. A year later, with their first collection, based on the idea of reconstruction, they won three prizes at the Salon Européen des Jeunes Stylistes at Hyères in France, at the Festival International de Mode et de Photographie. The collection consisted of ten looks and was partly made from old suits and shirts cut up and restitched together, some distorted by over-large linings, and one patterned with distressed sequins intended to leave a trail of silver. For their second collection, Viktor & Rolf duplicated a dress found in a flea market, and then subjected the new dress to a series of abortive experiments, more akin to a performance than a fashion collection: slamming it in a door, cutting it, burning it, 'amputating' it and appliquéing lace 'stains'.

Viktor & Rolf then began to produce fashion installations in galleries in Europe, starting with *L'Hiver de l'Amour* at the Musée d'Art Moderne de la Ville de Paris in February 1994. These featured art references that played compulsively on fashion themes, expressing Viktor & Rolf's desire to be in the fashion world as creatives. The designers always referred to the shows as collections, using the traditional fashion nomenclature for each season: Spring/Summer or Autumn/Winter, followed by the year, always shown six months ahead of the actual date. The exhibition venues were prestigious, and Viktor & Rolf rapidly acquired a reputation as top-end conceptual designers who generated images and ideas rather than commercial fashion.

Like conceptual art, conceptual fashion took concepts and ideas as its raw materials. Unlike conceptual art, conceptual fashion was linked to the emergence of deconstruction fashion in the late 1980s and early 1990s, in particular to such Antwerp designers as Martin Margiela, and to the Japanese designers Yohji Yamamoto and Comme des Garçons. Deconstruction was anti-glamour and relied on a 'poor' aesthetic and innovative cut recognizable only to a cultural elite.[1] Conceptual fashion was also characterized by radically new retail spaces, experimental fashion shows and adventurous publishing ventures. Such work began to be seen in micro-zines (independent fashion magazines produced in small runs) and galleries across world cities. *Visionaire*, a quarterly 'magazine', used the format of the artist's book to commission conceptual designers to make experimental work, issued in limited editions and priced accordingly, costing anything from £70 to £350 per issue. Like the London magazine *Dazed & Confused*, *Visionaire* had a gallery, in this case in New York, where Viktor & Rolf showed in May 1999.

The Widow (White), 1997
Photograph: Inez van Lamsweerde and Vinoodh Matadin
Hair and make-up: James Kaliardos
Published in *Connaissance des arts*, February 2001

Where most conceptual fashion designers deconstructed generic garment types, as with Comme des Garçons' frayed seams worn on the outside in the 1980s, or, in the 1990s, Margiela's jackets that mimicked paper patterns and tailor's dummies, Viktor & Rolf, by contrast, have deconstructed the fashion industry. Only their first two collections tapped into the distressed aesthetic of avant-garde fashion. Since then, their clothes, unlike those of the Belgian and Japanese designers, have become increasingly referential. In their first couture collection, Spring/Summer 1998, one dress in vintage Yves Saint Laurent fabric incorporated visibly the selvedge bearing the YSL name, a homage to tradition translated into a modern idiom. In the 'Black Hole' ready-to-wear collection for Autumn/Winter 2001–02, Viktor & Rolf took inspiration from the signature silhouettes made famous by Chanel, Balenciaga and Yves Saint Laurent. From this period on, they began to develop a repertoire of garment 'types', such as the tuxedo and the white shirt, to which they added such decorative elements as frills and pussy-cat bows. The clothes have become increasingly prim. Witness, for example, Viktor & Rolf's play on conservative Parisian fashion clichés in their 'Silver' collection (Autumn/Winter 2006–07), with its 1950s references: neat day dresses, formal grey suits, flared trench coats and trim cocktail frocks, all with what the journalist Sarah Mower called 'that slightly queasy, mummified touch'.[2]

First couture collection, Spring/Summer 1998

Yet this prim quality is misleading. While Viktor & Rolf have drawn on a very different aesthetic in dress, they share with deconstruction an analytical and polemical attitude to fashion. The journalist Amy Spindler observed in 2000: 'It isn't just that Viktor & Rolf make exquisitely beautiful, clever clothes. It's that they're the first designers to comment so intelligently on the fashion industry even as they're participating in it, even revolutionizing it.'[3] Thus their early installations were critiques and commentaries on the industry and how hard it is to break in to, the over-scaled dresses of their first designs, in 1993, expressing, they said, how small they felt in the forbidding world of Paris fashion. *L'Apparence du Vide* was an installation in October 1995 at the Galerie Patricia Dorfmann in Paris. It consisted of five garments in gaudy gold lamé suspended from the ceiling, each matched by its shadow equivalent in black organza lying on the floor beneath. Irked at the lack of mainstream press response to this show, for their next collection, in 1996, Viktor & Rolf produced nothing at all, simply sending fashion editors a poster that read 'Viktor & Rolf on strike', with which they also fly-posted Paris. In all their early collections, Viktor & Rolf operated as fashion designers in waiting, for at this stage they produced no commercial collections.

Viktor & Rolf's *Launch* at the Torch Gallery in Amsterdam in October 1996 marked the culmination of their period of producing installations rather than fashion shows. It embodied their hopes for the future in miniature. Having no money for a catwalk show, they created a microcosm of a fashion launch, with all the paraphernalia required to set up a fashion house but without the investment: a miniature catwalk, boutique, photo studio, atelier and a campaign for a fictional Viktor & Rolf perfume. This included a set of life-size perfume bottles similar to that of Chanel No. 5, each sealed shut; a photograph; and a press release. That the unopenable bottles sold for a considerable sum was part of the concept. A reference to Marcel Duchamp's *Air de Paris* (1919), the gesture also brought to mind Piero Manzoni's ninety tins of *Artist's Shit*, weighed, canned and priced according to the current gold rate in May 1961. That Viktor & Rolf were aware of this generation of artists is suggested by other references to the immaterial (the 'Long Live the Immaterial' or 'Bluescreen' collection, Autumn/Winter 2002–03) and the void (*L'Apparence du Vide*) that invoke the work of Yves Klein. *Saut dans le vide* (Leap into the Void), the photo Klein published in a mock edition of the *Journal du dimanche* on 27 November 1960, was, like a Viktor & Rolf show, a kind of wish-event staged for the camera.

After *Launch*, Viktor & Rolf began to produce actual shows, and the next period of their career was marked by five consecutive 'couture' collections. They held their first couture fashion show during Paris Fashion Week in January 1998, in the Galerie Thaddaeus Ropac, albeit without the endorsement of the Chambre Syndicale de la Haute Couture, which regulates and protects the status of haute couture. Relying on image and scenography, each of Viktor & Rolf's couture shows developed a strong element of performance that also characterized their earlier work. For the first couture show, the models clambered on to a plinth and posed like statues, one, in a columnar white dress, removing her white porcelain hat and giant necklace and throwing them to the ground, where they shattered into fragments. For the 'Russian Doll' collection for Autumn/Winter 1999–2000, the petite model Maggie Rizer revolved on a turntable while the two designers came and went with increasingly heavy, crystal-encrusted jute garments, which they carefully fitted on her, building up the layers like a Russian *matrioshka* doll.

'Catwalk' (detail), from *Launch*, 1996

More breathtaking, even, than the stagecraft and conceptual innovations of these early shows was Viktor & Rolf's commercial chutzpah. What they produced might best be described as stealth fashion that slipped in under the fashion radar. For, despite their materiality on the catwalk, the clothes barely existed outside the phantasmagoric realm of the fashion show. As noted in *Black + White Magazine* in 2000, 'The design duo has actually produced a severely limited number of clothes. Their gowns tend to go straight from the catwalks into art museums rather than into wardrobes.' *Harper's Bazaar* also reported that 'the number of Viktor & Rolf outfits sold to women who actually wear them comes to a grand total of three. Carefully, cleverly, even poetically, they have spent years crafting their image.'[4]

In 2000 Didier Grumbach, president of the Chambre Syndicale de la Haute Couture, commented that Viktor & Rolf were among the first, after Thierry Mugler and Jean Paul Gaultier, to return to a couture calendar: 'They were not admitted [to the Chambre Syndicale] straight away for the simple reason that, outside the circle of the initiated who had awarded them the prize at the Hyères Festival, no one knew their collections as they were still "virtual". Their multimedia [i.e. press and PR] success instantly changed that situation.'[5] In other words, it was enough to produce immaterial meaning so long as it became real in the media. Like an audacious bluff, through the very act of anticipating and staging their entry on to the fashion scene, Viktor & Rolf effected it for real. And so, despite not conforming to any of the Chambre's requirements and despite selling to museums rather than couture clients, Viktor & Rolf were invited to become a guest member of the Chambre in July 1999. The designers themselves commented:

We've never been quite sure if we would live up to the fashion world's strict rules and requirements. While infiltrating the business with our ideas, we've worked hard to maintain our love for fashion … Media coverage is essential to understanding our engagements with the fashion world through the last years. We have always been fascinated by the press we get (and lack of it!) – perhaps because our work seems to exist only once it has been published. The media breathes life into fashion![6]

Viktor & Rolf thus put their finger on the role and importance of image in a media-driven culture. Susan Sontag has argued that, in the modern period, our perception of reality is shaped by the type and frequency of images we perceive. Observing that, from the mid-nineteenth century, image and illusion became a new form of reality, she cites the nineteenth-century German philosopher

Ludwig Feuerbach: 'Our era prefers the image to the thing, the copy to the original, the representation to the reality, appearance to being.'[7] Today, this observation gains new meaning, with the advent of new digital technology and vastly accelerated cycles of consumption, particularly in fashion. Viktor & Rolf themselves observed in 1999 that 'fashion doesn't have to be something people wear. Fashion is also an image.'[8] Their 'Bluescreen' collection was a vivid illustration of this, using a video camera linked to a computer and a video projector to record models as they moved down the catwalk. Images from urban and natural landscapes were added by the computer and were projected on two large screens placed on either side of the catwalk, further blurring the distinction between image and reality.

Viktor & Rolf are semiotic tacticians. Image and presentation are fundamental to their work, and self-reference is at the core of it. They have appropriated the reflexive personae of the art world and used them in high fashion. They are smooth operators along the lines of both Andy Warhol and Gilbert & George, and their deadpan, doppelgänger self-presentation suggests that they know they are 'product'. Multilingual and media savvy, carefully co-ordinated and increasingly similar in appearance, they have engineered themselves a role in many of their shows, from tapdancing ('There's no Business like Show Business' collection, Spring/Summer 2001) to modelling their first menswear collection ('Monsieur', Autumn/Winter 2003–04). Precisely because their work is all about image, commercial success is no bar to showmanship and spectacular scenography. Unlike other experimental or conceptual designers, Viktor & Rolf have not had to tone down their presentation as they move into the mainstream. In *The Society of the Spectacle* in the 1960s, Guy Debord argued that consumer culture was so pervasive that it recuperated – that is, it commodified – every revolutionary gesture the instant it was made.[9] Viktor & Rolf's shows and collections retain their celluloid quality as a form of beautiful deception that can masquerade as revolution and recuperation all at once. They both revel in the 'society of the spectacle' and reveal it. They share with Warhol an ability to exist simultaneously inside and outside consumer culture: they love it and luxuriate in it, but at the same time they offer a knowing commentary on it.

'Monsieur', Autumn/Winter 2003–04

In March 2000 Viktor & Rolf finally moved into manufacturing with their first ready-to-wear collection, 'Stars & Stripes' (Autumn/Winter 2000–01). But they staged one more couture collection, their fifth, 'Bells' (Autumn/Winter 2000–01), in July. Dreamy and evocative, 'Bells' presented 'aural fashion', the models' garments announcing by the tinkling of tiny bells stitched all over them their imminent arrival in a fog-filled hall. By contrast, 'Stars & Stripes' was brash, both in appearance and in spirit. The designers described the ready-to-wear collection as 'our ode to commercialism, our ambition to become a big, global brand.'[10] Soon enough it was featured on the front of the *New York Times* fashion magazine. At that stage Viktor & Rolf introduced their logo, the intaglio sealing-wax disc embossed with the letters 'V&R' that has since appeared on all their merchandising. In 2003 they launched 'Monsieur', their menswear range, and designed a capsule collection of seven pieces for the French mail-order catalogue La Redoute. In October 2004 they used the show for their ready-to-wear 'Flowerbomb' collection (Spring/Summer 2005) to launch their first perfume in association with L'Oréal, thus fulfilling the promise of *Launch* staged eight years earlier. In April 2005 they opened their first shop (another feature of *Launch*) in Milan's exclusive retail district, the Quadrilatero d'oro; that year they also developed a range of Viktor & Rolf eyewear for the Far Eastern market. The next year, during the show for their 'Ballroom' collection (Spring/Summer 2007), they launched Antidote, their men's fragrance, and in November, following in the footsteps of Karl Lagerfeld and Stella McCartney, designed a range for the international fast-fashion chain H&M.

Viktor & Rolf could not, it seems, have moved faster from the margins to the mainstream. Theirs is a back-to-front career path in the sense that it is more common for designers to start out in commercial fashion and only later to find their work endorsed by museum curators in international exhibitions. A sense of inversion and reversal also finds expression in much of their design work. The 'Upside Down' collection (Spring/Summer 2006) was quite literally back-to-front, a show that had finished before it even began. Opening with the two designers taking their final bow on the catwalk, the show ran against a backdrop of an upside-down 'V&R' logo and a soundtrack of Diana Ross singing 'Upside Down' in reverse. Moving on to the final parade of clapping models, the show then wound backwards through a collection of upside-down clothes featuring sleeves as trousers, bustier bodices as skirts.

There's no Business like Show Business,
Spring/Summer 2001

In this collection the upside-down and back-to-front elements were literal, as they were in the Viktor & Rolf shop in Milan, an upside-down interior by Siebe Tettero based on a traditional Parisian couture salon. In more diffuse ways, all their work has an upside-down or distorted quality. Viktor & Rolf have played with scale, and have layered, altered, exaggerated and repeated traditional design elements and motifs, often drawing on the visual language of 'classic' fashion, such as Chanel's juxtaposition of black and white or black and pale pink. These and other familiar design features have been submitted to various forms of distortion to create, for example, high collars, giant cuffs and elaborate draping. The clothes may then be further embellished with exaggerated and over-scaled accessories that refer to, but alter, classic fashion accessories and trims.

Running through all Viktor & Rolf's work is a play on opposites and contrasts, as they ricochet between male and female, sad and happy, or black and white. The 'Flowerbomb' collection was a typical example. It opened with black-clad models in shiny black motorcycle helmets walking to a rock soundtrack. The models took their position in a *tableau vivant* reminiscent of Loomis Dean's photograph of 1957 of Christian Dior models. Next there was an explosion in the dark at the end of the catwalk, after which the set revolved 180 degrees to reveal the same tableau, but this time in pink and gold. From this set, the individual models detached themselves one after another and walked the catwalk to romantic music. 'Flowerbomb' flipped from menace into soft-focus celebration. Each of the pink garments mirrored one of the black ones, just as the suspended gold dresses in the installation *L'Apparence du Vide* had been echoed by their shadowy black organza counterparts on the floor.

Viktor & Rolf's work is galvanized by such contrasts, from their 'Black Hole' collection, in which black-clad models processed along the catwalk with black-painted faces and hands, to the 'White' collection that followed it (Spring/Summer 2002), based on the Holy Communion. The designers have sometimes shown a collection twice during the same show to reveal two different facets. The 'Atomic Bomb' collection (Autumn/Winter 1998–99) was staged first with voluminous padding worn under the clothes to create a distorted silhouette, and then again with the padding removed in order to show the drape effect of the 'deflated' garment. The 'Black Light' collection (Spring/Summer 1999) was made entirely in black-and-white fabric, and it too was shown twice, first in black ultraviolet light, in which only the white silk gazar showed up – a frill, a bow or a disembodied skeleton gliding down the catwalk – and then in white light, which revealed an entire collection based around the tuxedo.

Black Light, Spring/Summer 1999

There is in all Viktor & Rolf's work an element of medieval carnival and the *commedia dell'arte* theme used by Elsa Schiaparelli in 1938. This became explicit in their 'Harlequin' collection (Spring/Summer 2008). Characterized by artifice and masquerade, carnival licenses social anarchy and symbolic inversion. In what the Soviet formalist critic Mikhail Bakhtin called the 'grotesque body of carnival', the outside and inside of bodies become confused.[11] The 'Atomic Bomb' collection saw the body made 'grotesque' by the stuffing of the clothes with padding, and the festive spirit was invoked by an oscillation between millennial doom and wild partying. Bakhtin argues that, in carnival, the mouth is a liminal space that breaches the border between inside and outside. 'Harlequin' suggested the interiority of the carnivalesque body, as the models walking on to the catwalk were dwarfed by the gigantic mouth of an enormous photograph by Inez van Lamsweerde and Vinoodh Matadin of the model Shalom Harlow, through which they emerged.

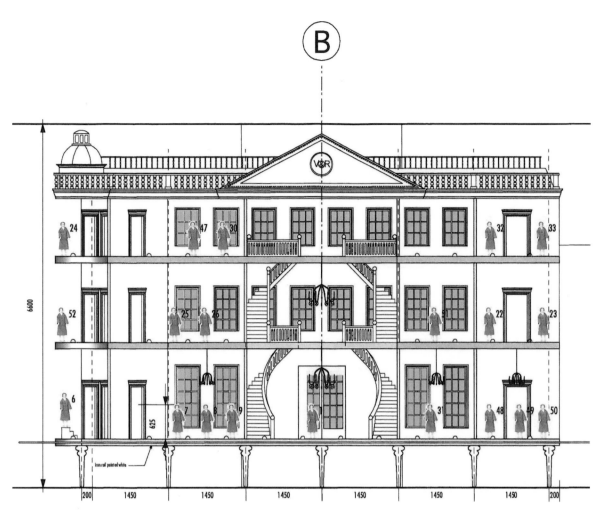

Barbican doll's house, front elevation
Design: Siebe Tettero. Drawing: Meike Stoetzer

As much as Viktor & Rolf's work invokes the symbolic inversion of carnival, it also recalls the looking-glass world of Lewis Carroll, in which nothing is quite as it seems. The 'Harlequin' collection's play on scale also characterizes their installation at the Barbican exhibition. Siebe Tettero has designed a 6-metre-high (19 ft 8 in.) doll's house in the centre of the gallery. The public can gaze at the doll's house from three different levels: from the ground, from a specially constructed viewing tower and from the upper floor of the gallery. Most of the rooms contain one or more dolls, each about 70 centimetres (27½ in.) high and dressed in an outfit from a Viktor & Rolf collection. Based on nineteenth-century antique dolls, re-created by a Belgian dollmaker, these miniature mannequins have real human hair, bisque porcelain faces and papier-mâché bodies. Moving past the giant doll's house into the upper gallery, the visitor encounters a series of rooms replicating those of the doll's house, now containing a human-size doll identical to its smaller version, right down to the outfit. In this way the visitor is miniaturized, Alice-in-Wonderland style, but can then 'grow' again by returning to the doll's house.

There are precedents for Viktor & Rolf's use of dolls and doll's houses. The Rijksmuseum in Amsterdam, where Viktor & Rolf live and work, contains three seventeenth-century cabinet houses, or doll's houses. One, known as the Doll's House of Petronella Oortman, and dated 1686–1710, stands 2.5 metres (8 ft 2½ in.) high. To view the upper storey, visitors mount a set of external steps not dissimilar to the viewing tower of the Barbican doll's house. An eighteenth-century painting of Petronella's doll's house, by Jacob Appel, shows it peopled by more than twenty fashionably dressed dolls, although only one (a baby doll) survives in the museum's collection today.

Jacob Appel
The Doll's House of Petronella Oortman,
1700–20

Seventeenth- and eighteenth-century European dressmakers sent small 'fashion dolls' round Europe to advertise their dressmaking talents; these were, in effect, the first fashion models. In 1946 the Chambre Syndicale de la Haute Couture hoped to revive its fortunes after the war by touring the 'Théâtre de la Mode', a collection of some two hundred elegant wire-framed dolls, each dressed and accessorized by a different Paris couturier. Fashion dolls were replaced in the nineteenth century by life-size wooden or wicker mannequins kept in the dressmakers' premises. These gave their name to the 'living mannequins' or models, who, from the second half of the century, gradually replaced them. The modern fashion model thus has as her predecessor first a miniature fashion doll, then a life-size dummy, both invoked in Viktor & Rolf's Barbican installation.

Viktor & Rolf's dolls have an uncanny quality all of their own. Originally made for adults, not children, fashion dolls were modelled like miniature adults. Viktor & Rolf's combine heads based on nineteenth-century dolls of the *bébé* type produced by Maison Jumeau in Paris, which, with their childish faces, were intended as children's toys, with bodies based on German lady dolls (or fashion dolls) popular between about 1860 and 1890 and reputedly used by couturiers to model dresses. Viktor & Rolf's figures are actually rather large for dolls of this period, and this too makes them somewhat alarming. For, as Susan Stewart argues in her book on miniaturization, quoting from Stanley Hall's study of dolls, 'to its reduced scale the doll world owes much of its charm. The cases of fear of dolls are almost always of large dolls.'[12] When scaled up to adult size, Viktor & Rolf's dolls, with their glassy eyes, are creepy in a different way, as they play on the difference between human and doll, animate and inanimate, life and death.

It is not the first time Viktor & Rolf have used dolls. There were the tiny dolls in *Launch*; the *matrioshka* revolving like a ballerina doll in a musical jewellery box in the 'Russian Doll' collection; the nineteenth-century Jumeau doll in 'One Woman Show' (Autumn/Winter 2003–04), where the models were identically made up with pale skin, red hair and no eyebrows as clones of the actress Tilda Swinton, who also modelled; and the marionette or ventriloquist's dummy in the first 'Monsieur', where the identically styled Viktor & Rolf appeared as uncanny doubles.

In his essay 'The Uncanny' (1919), Sigmund Freud described both human doubles and dolls as potentially uncanny: the double poses a challenge to the idea of individuality, and the doll straddles an uncomfortable boundary between the living and the dead.[13] Freud's essay opens with a semantic analysis of the German word for the uncanny, *unheimlich*, and its opposite, *heimlich* ('homely'), and from there proceeds to the idea that the uncanny arises when something both unfamiliar and hidden is revealed. Here the punning title of the Barbican exhibition, *The House of Viktor & Rolf*, comes into play. The Barbican doll's house is modelled on the couture house rather than the domestic interior, and shares the *unheimlich* ('unhomely') quality of the uncanny. For the house of Viktor and Rolf is not a home but a fashion house, in which all sorts of other reversals are possible, too.

At the dollmaker's, spring 2008

Viktor & Rolf achieve their effects by surreal juxtapositions: an adult next to a same-size doll, or a miniaturized fashion model emerging on to a catwalk through a gigantic mouth. In *The House of Viktor & Rolf* at the Barbican, the viewer moves from a tiny world to a gigantic one. A visitor who imagined her- or himself experiencing events in the two sizes of doll's house would be mentally shifted from human size to doll size and back again. Susan Stewart argues that doll's houses produce 'miniature time', whereby, through its reduction in scale, the miniature is displaced from everyday space and time to an 'infinite time of reverie'.[14] She cites research in which miniaturized environments were shown to affect people's experience of the duration of time, a smaller space producing the sense of time passing faster: 'In other words, miniature time transcends the duration of everyday life.'[15] If the duration of time is initially contracted in Viktor & Rolf's doll's house for the Barbican, the human visitor having mentally had to shrink to 70 centimetres tall, how much might it subsequently expand in the gallery's rooms, where the same visitor is confronted by a human-size doll in a scaled-up room?

The oscillation of scale in the Barbican show, with its concomitant distortion of time and space, evokes an earlier moment in the Viktor & Rolf story: the miniature *Launch* of 1996. All their subsequent collections have been a way of materializing the prediction they made in that installation. By willing a fashion house into being, and by dint of determination as much as talent, they made it happen over the following ten years. The tiny installation can thus be seen as a charm or a form of imitative magic that made a wish come true: it conjured up the phantasmagoric brand of Viktor & Rolf. The large Barbican doll's house evidences Viktor & Rolf's desire to visualize their world as they have created it over the last fifteen years. But what if it too is nothing less than a charm or wish emblem, a model in miniature of their future couture house, just as *Launch* was a model for their future business? For, if a miniaturized fashion launch can be so effective, what might the far larger Barbican installation be capable of conjuring up – a fully fledged salon on the rue du Faubourg Saint-Honoré or the rue de la Paix, the historic home of haute couture? In the era of late capitalism and globalization, Viktor & Rolf bring magical thinking bang up to date.[16] Freud believed that children expect their dolls to come to life: 'The idea of a "living doll" excites no fear at all.'[17] If the dolls in the Barbican came to life, what might they not do? With career ambitions to match those of their makers, they may even now be planning their future in the powerhouse of Viktor & Rolf.

1. See Alison Gill, 'Deconstruction Fashion: The Making of Unfinished, Decomposing and Re-assembled Clothes', *Fashion Theory*, vol. 2, no. 1 (March 1998), pp. 25–49; Harold Koda, 'Rei Kawakubo and the Aesthetic of Poverty', *Costume: Journal of the Costume Society of America*, vol. 11 (1985), pp. 5–10; Ingrid Loschek, 'The Deconstructionists', in *Icons of Fashion: The 20th Century*, ed. Gerda Buxbaum (Munich, London and New York: Prestel, 1999), pp. 146–47; Richard Martin, 'Destitution and Deconstruction: The Riches of Poverty in the Fashion of the 1990s', *Textile & Text*, vol. 15, no. 2 (1992), pp. 3–8.

2. Sarah Mower, 'Runway Review: Viktor & Rolf, Fall 2006 Ready-to-Wear', style.com (accessed 23 November 2007).

3. *Viktor & Rolf Haute Couture Book*, exhib. cat. by Amy Spindler and Didier Grumbach (Groningen, Groninger Museum, 2000), p. 6.

4. Jonathan Turner, 'Dutch Courage', *Black + White Magazine*, no. 45 (September 2000); William Middleton, 'New Amsterdam', *Harper's Bazaar* (May 2000).

5. *Viktor & Rolf Haute Couture Book*, p. 5.

6. *E-Magazine: Viktor & Rolf par Viktor & Rolf, première décennie*, exhib. cat. (Paris, Musée de la Mode et du Textile, 2003), p. 13.

7. Susan Sontag, *On Photography* (Harmondsworth: Penguin Books, 1979), p. 153.

8. Viktor & Rolf, quoted in Stephen Gan, *Visionaire's Fashion 2001: Designers of the New Avant-Garde*, ed. Alix Browne (London: Laurence King, 1999), n.p.

9. Guy Debord, *The Society of the Spectacle* [1967], trans. Donald Nicholson-Smith (New York: Zone Books, 1994).

10. Viktor & Rolf, quoted in *Viktor & Rolf: 'Because We're Worth It!' The Making of a Fashion House*, documentary directed by Femke Wolting (2005), distrib. Submarine Channel, The Netherlands.

11. Mikhail Bakhtin, *Rabelais and His World* [1968], trans. Hélène Iswolsky (Bloomington: Indiana University Press, 1984). I am indebted to Francesca Granata, whose doctoral research at Central Saint Martins College of Art and Design, University of the Arts London, has informed this interpretation.

12. Stanley G. Hall, *A Study of Dolls* (New York: E.L. Kellogg & Co., 1897), quoted in Susan Stewart, *On Longing: Narratives of the Miniature, the Gigantic, the Souvenir, the Collection* (Durham, NC: Duke University Press, 1993), p. 124.

13. Sigmund Freud, 'The Uncanny' [1919], in *Works: The Standard Edition of the Complete Psychological Works of Sigmund Freud*, general ed. James Strachey, vol. 17 (London: Hogarth Press, 1955), pp. 234–36.

14. Stewart, *On Longing*, p. 65.

15. The experiment was conducted by the School of Architecture at the University of Tennessee. See Alton J. DeLong, 'Phenomenological Space-Time: Towards an Experimental Relativity', *Science*, vol. 213 (1981), cited in Stewart, *On Longing*, p. 66. The experiment identified a 'phenomenological correlation between the experience of scale and the experience of duration'. Researchers asked adult subjects to imagine themselves experiencing events in three different scaled models at 1:6, 1:12 and 1:24, and to say when they felt they had been engaged in these activities for thirty minutes. The results showed that the duration of time was compressed to the same scale as the environment, so that thirty minutes would be experienced in five minutes at 1:12 and in two-and-a-half minutes at 1:24.

16. Magical thinking is a term used by Western anthropologists to describe non-Western belief systems and structures of representation. It is analogical rather than logical, imitative rather than scientific, and reverses cause and effect. Voodoo dolls are an example of magical thinking. The term was used by Joan Didion in *The Year of Magical Thinking* (New York: Alfred A. Knopf, 2005) to describe her experience of mourning. The logic of magical thinking permeates much structuralist thought as well as psychoanalysis, with its emphasis on underlying or hidden meanings that are revealed in the condensed symbolism and imagery of, for example, dreams, slips, jokes and errors.

17. Freud, 'The Uncanny', p. 223.

White Collection SS 02
Look Madelaine

Photograph: Inez van Lamsweerde and Vinoodh Matadin, 2002

In the autumn of 1996, two barely known Dutch fashion designers working under the name of Viktor & Rolf showed their *Launch* collection not on the catwalk but at the Torch Gallery in Amsterdam. The collection was crafted entirely in miniature, mimicking the 'Théâtre de la Mode', a set of hand-made dolls roughly one-third life-size and dressed in original couture designs that travelled the world in 1946 to advertise the wares of Paris ateliers struggling to survive fabric rationing and the aftermath of the German occupation. Fifty years on, Viktor Horsting and Rolf Snoeren were more penniless still, but this was a time when the power of designer fashion – and the global brand in particular – had reached its zenith. With this in mind, Viktor & Rolf had it all mapped out. Alongside the small but perfectly formed clothes themselves, *Launch* included a mini-design studio, catwalk, photo shoot, boutique and, perhaps most famously, a life-size, limited-edition perfume bottle notable for the fact that it was sealed tight and therefore could not be opened.

Today, Viktor & Rolf have realized their lifelong dream of becoming fashion designers in their own right, showing a full-size collection in Paris twice yearly, and with a bestselling women's perfume, Flowerbomb, and a men's fragrance, Antidote, under their belts. It seems not insignificant that, on the occasion of their first retrospective in the United Kingdom, the designers have chosen to go back to their roots, offering up perhaps the most glamorous doll's house in history, peopled with Viktor & Rolf-clad dolls. They explain:

We wanted to create a new world. Using dolls is like taking control. When we had just started out we created a series of miniature installations visualizing our strongest ambitions: a doll on a catwalk, a doll in a photo studio, a miniature boutique and so forth. The dolls were an abstraction of people, and the scenes they enacted showed a life we desired but dared only to dream of. Looking at that life from a distance, fantasizing about it in a suggestion of play – as serious as these adult toys were – instead of really living it, seemed to be the closest we could get to the realization of our dreams.

Viktor & Rolf's return to a miniature format for the current exhibition also reflects a certain caution with regard to the 'retrospective' tag. For fashion designers in particular, dedicated as they must be, at least to some extent, to the shock of the new, this is always a double-edged sword:

Ten years down the line our first thought turned to these dolls when we thought of a 'retrospective'. We felt a strong need to do something that related to our old work, to use it and make it a part of a new story, a bigger one, to turn it into something new – and also something homogeneous maybe. By showing all of this together in a doll's house, as if it were one big projection of the future or, better maybe, a retro-vision of the future, we try to edit our own past and put a spell on our fates. It was also clear to us from the start that we wanted to use the exhibition to create new work, outside of the context and conditions of the fashion system.

If the scaling-down of size is an integral part of the Viktor & Rolf story, creating clothing that is larger than life is equally significant. From tuxedo jackets overblown to resemble mushroom clouds for the 'Atomic Bomb' collection (Autumn/Winter 1998–99) to dresses that comprised a single pink silk bow of Brobdingnagian proportions (the 'Flowerbomb' collection, Spring/Summer 2005) and, of course, the 'Russian Doll' collection (Autumn/Winter 1999– 2000), for which the model Maggie Rizer was dressed in no fewer than nine layers, one on top of another, by the designers' own fair hands, this too has been a central part of their œuvre. Viktor & Rolf scale up the proportions of clothing steeped in the French tradition, thereby not only reflecting the vulnerability of the wearer, who seems small in her clothes, but also, conversely, magnifying both the power of the wearer in view of their sheer size and that of fashion in a broader sense:

It started out with our very first collection – the one we designed for the contest in Hyères in 1993. We had just moved to Paris and were living in dismal conditions: a shoebox of an apartment, shared among three people. We had very little money and no employment. We had moved there to try our luck and to be closer to our ideal of fashion and of what it means to be a fashion designer. Being in Paris seemed to be a part of that. We were just out of school and were floating in free air. This was both exhilarating and difficult, because without a frame of reference, one is left to one's own devices – or each other's in our case. The first collection felt like a scream for attention, and it set a standard for the rest of our work. We started working on layering and, automatically, exaggerated volumes came about. The exaggeration was a reaction to a sense of loneliness and insignificance that was caused by our first encounter with Paris – Paris the city, and Paris the capital of fashion, and the bastion we wanted to storm. We felt like we were David against Goliath, and have retained that feeling ever since.

above:
Viktor during 'Viktor & Rolf on strike', Paris, 1996

opposite:
Drawings for Hyères, 1993

Viktor Horsting and Rolf Snoeren grew up in the Dutch provinces, far from an obviously fashion-friendly environment. (V: 'I had two working parents. I am the middle one of three brothers.' R: 'The same, except that I am the youngest of three brothers.') Both were nonetheless instinctively drawn from a very early age to the iconography of fashion and to certain main players, drawing constantly, particularly in a figurative style, and focusing specifically on women and their clothes.

We always loved to draw and paint. I [Viktor] would constantly draw women and dresses, even as a little child. When I was a teenager, I became fascinated with certain images and a certain aesthetic that I didn't recognize as fashion or fashionable at first, I just thought they were beautiful: Steve Strange, Serge Lutens, Mathilde Willink, Guy Bourdin. I was fascinated by make-up and slowly started to understand that there was a world called fashion. In my imagination, this became something magical. I had very little access to the media and would spend a lot of time daydreaming up my own version of fashion, inspired by the few images I saw. I am convinced that a lack of information has been crucial to our development, as creative teenagers and as fledgling Dutch fashion designers. The lack of images fuelled our imaginations. There was just no information on how to do anything! So we invented it ourselves – sometimes wasting time, reinventing the wheel, but also making up our own minds as to what fashion could be to us.

Viktor & Rolf's designs are indebted primarily to the French haute couture tradition, their styles and volumes reflecting the work of the great Parisian couture houses, including Schiaparelli, Chanel, Balenciaga and, most prominently, Yves Saint Laurent. However, the fact that, unlike the aforementioned big names, they grew up in an environment where there was little actual fashion to be seen, remains central to their philosophy:

We have a love–hate relationship with our roots. Our nation is lacking in cosmopolitan culture and society, while we grew up longing for glamour, sophistication and style. We are not consciously taking inspiration from our country's history. To say to what extent our Dutchness influences our work is like trying to see one's own eye: it is impossible. But it is the very lack of fashion in our country (no media, no industry, no artistic or cultural centre), the absence of an example or a forerunner, that made us conjure up a dream world of fashion when we were kids, and caused us to think about our work more freely maybe than if we had been exposed to fashion as an integrated part of society, as in France or Italy, say. We just had to find out for ourselves, and maybe this was refreshing sometimes.

> Although Viktor & Rolf were diligent students, their memory of their schooldays is one of 'repression and boredom'.

V: I had interests that were a paradox, some more expected (and accepted) and some more unusual for a teenage boy. I was good at school and went to the conservatoire to study the violin. But I also constantly drew dresses in my notebooks and was fascinated with make-up and fashion images. I never felt unpopular. I just wasn't interested. But I did have a hard time reconciling my 'unusual' side with the outside world myself. There was no one to share my passion with, so I ended up being quite solitary.

R: I did not feel unpopular either, but I did feel alienated from my environment. I knew I would leave as soon as possible and, although I was a quiet boy, I wasn't very insecure. I just wasn't really interested.

> The world of fashion, though still accessible only through the media and books, represented something of a sanctuary for both designers, who felt – and it is a familiar story – that they would find themselves more able to relate to this world, famed as it is for prizing individuality, than to the one in which they grew up.

Viktor (below) and Rolf (right) in their Paris apartment, 1995

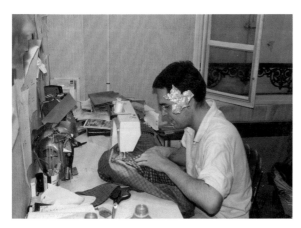

Zwaantje and Vicky, Rolf and Viktor's dogs, 2008　　　　Rolf and Viktor, 2003

V: I had developed a profound interest in fashion from a very early age, to the point that I was sure that I wanted to be close to this kind of world. Most of all, I wanted to encounter people with the same interests, passions and tastes because I was tired of feeling alone. For a long time, Karl Lagerfeld was my source of inspiration and my hero. I had read in an interview that he went to Paris at fourteen to study fashion, so anything other than that seemed out of the question for me. It reconfirmed what had already been instilled in me through my own upbringing: that one has to strive for the best, and one has an obligation to fulfil one's talents. 'Fame can be bought with sweat', my violin teacher used to say to me. Studying in Paris seemed impossible, but it was within my reach to apply for the best fashion education in The Netherlands at that time: Arnhem. Going to art school to become a fashion designer instead of to the conservatoire to become a violinist was not an easy decision to make, even though the choice was simple. I just didn't have the same passion for music as I had for fashion.

R: I had a naïve ambition to become famous, to be noticed. I thought briefly about acting, but, as I was always drawing alone in my room, I decided I was better suited to becoming a fashion illustrator. While studying fashion I noticed that drawing was too limiting for me. I was looking for the total experience.

Then, as now, Arnhem Academy of Art and Design had a reputation for being home to the most respected fashion department in the country. In particular, the designers explain:

There is a strong focus on personal artistic development, and we were encouraged to question every aspect of design. A conceptual approach to fashion was *bon ton* at that time in our group. It was a trend in general. Technique was an important part of the course. There was a strong conviction that you had to be acquainted with every aspect of the design process. There was no link to the industry or the media, however, and our education seemed to take place in a vacuum.

For *Visionaire*, no. 17, 1995

Nonetheless, as self-proclaimed 'children of the 1980s', Viktor & Rolf did focus their attention on the fashion superpowers of that era: Comme des Garçons, Thierry Mugler, Yves Saint Laurent. Above all, however, Arnhem was where the designers first met each other, immediately establishing the close friendship that, over and above anything else, has been key to the realization of their dreams:

We met in 1988 when we were applying to study. We then became good friends at school. We felt the same drive and ambition and, somehow, a personal connection that we could not yet define at that moment. We just really liked each other and enjoyed each other's company. Both of us were away from home for the first time, living by ourselves, doing what we liked to do instead of attending a boring high school. For the first time, we were in an environment where being openly gay was a possibility. Our tastes, style and ambition were on the same level. We seemed to be attracted to fashion in a similar way. Of course, this is a process of discovery, but we recognized a similar sensibility right away. It is as if a part of our core is made out of the same material.

Heading straight for Paris – the fashion capital of the world – immediately after graduation, Viktor & Rolf must have had quite a shock when they found that, having been the stars of the show in their home country, in France they were nowhere and nobody. The story of their early days in that city reflects the bohemian artist of twentieth-century folklore: think everyone from James Joyce to Henry Miller and, in terms of fashion specifically, John Galliano:

We had moved to Paris on an instinct. We sub-let a tiny apartment in the 20th arrondissement, seven flights of stairs without an elevator, together with a friend of ours. Viktor's dad dropped us off, had a coffee and went on his way. We unpacked, sat down at the only table in the place and started to draw. This was 1 December 1992. It all sounds very *La Bohème*, and it was. No electricity; candles, bread and red wine. The real reason we were in Paris was to try to work for a big house, to be close to the real world and gain experience. We could only dream of starting our own label. We considered working on our collection as a side project, but an important one. Slowly, bit by bit, the side project moved into the spotlight. From the very beginning, we did not consciously divide work. Roughly, we would both work on the same things. We would do everything ourselves: the patterns – which were as big as the floor of the apartment, the apartment being quite small and the patterns quite big – the garments … Everything went from one of us to the other, depending on time, energy, affinity or degree of back pain!

The notion of the superstar fashion designer characterized fashion in the late twentieth century: from the afore-mentioned Galliano to Tom Ford, the personality of the creative director pervades an entire brand. But it is interesting to note that Viktor & Rolf always saw themselves as a unit, as one designer. 'In our case it works. We are aware that it is special and unique. In our case 1+1=3', they state. It is small wonder that comparisons are continually drawn with Gilbert & George.

Viktor & Rolf's collection in 1993 for the Salon Européen des Jeunes Stylistes at Hyères in southern France won them the event's three most important fashion prizes and brought them to the attention of the global fashion fraternity. They said at the time that the 'extreme silhouettes and multiple layers, concealing and disfiguring the wearer's body, express the alienation we felt in the "City of Fashion"'. Now they remember:

The absence of any security or prospect, of means and space, brought about a profound sense of loneliness caused by an absence of friends or family and no vision of our future. We didn't think about a wearer for one minute during that period. We created our first collections as autonomous pieces, to express these emotions through the effect of clothes, styling and music. The presentation – be it catwalk show, exhibition or otherwise – was the end product. Even though we paid a lot of attention to their execution – technique has always been important to us – the clothes were designed to be looked at rather than to be worn.

While life in Paris was doubtless challenging, the culture of French fashion provided Viktor & Rolf with a rich web of references that continue to inform their work today. However, they initially attempted to strip their work of anything historical, starting, in the manner of Rei Kawakubo of Comme des Garçons, 'from zero'. In this, their method was more in line with that of conceptual artists than it was with that of traditional fashion designers. They explain:

Especially in the beginning, we made experiments trying to create 'without references'. We had the idea that we had to go to our core, to be 'real' and express creative authenticity with an absence of outer influences. We came to realize, as many before us, that this was a dead end. Instinctively, we had used historical references from the very beginning. In our first collection, for example, we showed a dress that consisted of fragments of a suit, sewn into a dress. We are, and always were, aware of history and want to use it to create something new.

As already seen, Viktor & Rolf's conceptual view of fashion was a result, at least in part, of an attempt to make as big an impact as possible with very limited resources. It is a measure of their strength – as well, of course, of their considerable wit – that in 1996, thoroughly disillusioned and disenchanted with their chosen career, in place of a conventional collection, they put up fly-posters all over the French fashion capital of a girl carrying a protest sign that read 'Viktor & Rolf on strike':

The strike was not aimed at the French fashion establishment in particular. It was directed at 'the fashion system' in general. We felt frustrated and couldn't seem to find our entrance into fashion. We were creating collections every season but on such a small and home-grown level that they stood in no relation to our ambitions. We simply didn't know how to realize these. Our ideas about fashion were just that: ideas. We were completely disconnected from the reality of the industry, from the market.

It is no secret that the British are particularly resistant to the idea of conceptual fashion. In the United Kingdom, clothes are clothes, and anything striving to express a bigger idea runs the risk of being labelled pretentious. And so Hussein Chalayan, for example, was never likely to be embraced as quickly as his contemporary, the more obviously pyrotechnic Alexander McQueen. Equally, in the late 1990s, Prada was less likely to appear in the news pages of British national papers than the more obviously accessible – and indeed overtly sexual – Gucci. Viktor & Rolf's work is exceptional in that it is clearly conceptual but also joyful, photogenic and unusually easy to read. Not only that, but, where other designers' concepts may be lost once the catwalk presentation is over and the clothes make the rails, with Viktor & Rolf the original idea runs through everything they touch:

We want the fashion to be judged as fashion, and it has to function as such. But on top of that we personally like to express more through our work than the evolution of a style or a way of dressing. We are constantly facing the challenge of finding the balance where the medium – that is clothes, fashion – does not get in the way of the message, but still has a right of existence in itself. We are torn between hope that we can stretch the medium and mould it into something we would like it to be – a means of expression beyond style – and exasperation that there are limits that we must accept, and that we are working within a system that we have to conform to, and at times really want to conform to.

From photo shoot for 'Viktor & Rolf on strike', Paris, 1996

In the beginning, any so-called limits were surmounted by the fact that, until the turn of the twenty-first century, Viktor & Rolf's collections were shown during the necessarily rarefied and proudly elitist haute couture season. Here clothing functions as a crucible for ideas, and nothing as pedestrian as budgetary constraint interferes with unbridled creativity and unparalleled craftsmanship:

We were drawn to couture and to its symbolic function. In fashion it is the top of the pyramid, the *ne plus ultra* of luxury. It also functions as a laboratory without commercial restraints. Couture is like a sacred realm outside reality – a notion we are quite inspired by. We actually made our disadvantage into our advantage, as we often try to do, realizing that, if we could make a name for ourselves in couture, at the highest level, the rest would follow. The 'Babushka' ['Russian Doll'] collection, where we dressed Maggie Rizer in nine consecutive layers on stage in Paris, is the best example of this vision. It was a performance, just to show a beautiful idea.

In the end, Viktor & Rolf's couture pieces were sold mainly to museums 'but Dodie Rosenkranz bought two outfits from our very first collection,' say the designers, 'a memory we cherish to this very day. We never considered our couture collections as wearable options, however, even though we paid extreme attention to fit, details and technical excellence – we hope. If a piece or a collection was finished, that was it for us. We considered them as sculptural pieces.'

In March 2000 Viktor & Rolf launched their career as ready-to-wear designers, taking as inspiration in their 'Stars & Stripes' collection (Autumn/Winter 2000–01) not the French fashion tradition but Americana, in particular the American flag, both celebrating and subverting their theme:

The first ready-to-wear collection had to be a clear departure from couture. We wanted to emphasize the difference between ready-to-wear and couture and not make a re-creation of a previous couture collection. At the same time, we wanted to express our ambition in fashion: to address people on a global scale and to become a luxury brand for the twenty-first century. To symbolize this global ambition, we searched for clothing icons that would be universally recognized: a sweatshirt, a pair of jeans, a classic tailored shirt. The Stars and Stripes were used as a symbol of expansion and a metaphor for our desire for omnipresence – equally tongue-in-cheek as genuine. All of this was juxtaposed with black wrappings that would partially or totally cover and distort the volumes of the basics underneath.

Then began the play between contrasts that characterizes designer ready-to-wear. These may seem obvious and even facile – black for autumn, white for summer, for example, or tweed in winter, flowers in spring – but Viktor & Rolf embraced them wholeheartedly. The 'Black Hole' collection (Autumn/Winter 2001–02), for example, was followed by the 'White' collection (Spring/Summer 2002). When the designers launched their first fragrance, they worked with both ends of the spectrum in the accompanying collection, and even the perfume's name, Flowerbomb, embodies that central contradiction:

Stars & Stripes, Autumn/Winter 2000–01

It's true that we are always searching for opposites. A certain tension makes things interesting for us. That's why Flowerbomb is such a good example. We invented the word ourselves. It's like an anti-weapon, a weapon to create beauty. We always strive for complexity. The world has become very two-dimensional and instant. But for us there is beauty in mystery, in being authentic. This can never be simplistic. We like it when something can be stupid and intelligent, romantic and aggressive all at the same time. Some people see more the ironic part of the work, others the more classical part. You can tap into different layers if you want to.

If, at the start of their career, Viktor & Rolf were placed firmly at the forefront of fashion's avant garde, they also showed an awareness of the need for a fashion designer working today to embrace not just the clothes themselves but, in addition, the marketing of a name, the art direction of an image and more. In this, they are the ultimate twenty-first-century designers:

From the beginning, we had a general feeling about our future, and we thought about fashion and our position within the fashion world in general terms, as a brand, if you will. We were aware that fashion has many elements apart from collections and shows. Beauty and perfume, for instance, have been on our map from a very early time, exemplified by the fake perfume. But we think that fashion can involve more than the elements we know today. Our background in the arts is an integral part of our identity and a place we are returning to occasionally. We would like to do more again in the future; it is new and has not been done yet. So we like to approach fashion as a broad medium that allows for many ways to express one's creativity. The brand we have created is a result of that approach. It functions like an umbrella. All of this came about naturally, by the way. We never made a plan or developed a strategy. It all just happened as a result of this vision we had, or maybe it was not even a vision, just a strong desire and an ideal, a need to express ourselves through fashion. We are quite reserved people and do not easily feel a connection to others. Our work serves as a tool to communicate and is quite charged in that sense.

The designers' need to express themselves through fashion, as they put it, reached its peak with the launch of their menswear line, 'Monsieur', in 2003. For this they not only modelled the collection on stage in Florence, but also created 'look books' featuring themselves as poster boys:

The idea was to emphasize two things: the collection was meant for us, for our kind of man – someone who has many paradoxes in life and needs to have a wardrobe to go with them, from casual to glamorous in a minute and often simultaneously. We also wanted to make a personal statement: namely, to express that we work as one designer, as one mind. There is no distinction between who does what. We don't think about what people 'need'. We think about what we would like to do or say, and try to understand whether there is some relevance to this message. A constant questioning of fashion itself as a system – and our own place in it – is always at the root of our work, as is the tension between doubts about our chosen medium, on the one hand, and the hope and desire to create something worthwhile, with beauty and meaning, on the other.

There are several shows that are landmarks for us: the 'Atomic Bomb' collection, as it was our breakthrough haute couture collection; also the 'Black Hole' collection, but it was a much bigger breakthrough because it was ready-to-wear and therefore available to a wider audience. But these two shows didn't give us the most pleasure; shows in general don't give pleasure but stress. One we did enjoy at the time was the 'Bluescreen' show [also known as 'Long Live the Immaterial', Autumn/Winter 2002–03], where we worked with the bluescreen effect. Two videos next to the catwalk replaced the blue clothes with moving images. Models were wearing, for example, a coat made from the sky and flying birds, or a dress made of film footage of Manhattan. For us it was mesmerizing to see the effect, something that we had not rehearsed and did not know what the end result would be.

Another show we found uplifting was the 'Flowerbomb' show, where we launched our first perfume. A podium with twenty-five black-clad models wearing black motorcycle helmets posed in a *tableau vivant* reminiscent of the famous Loomis Dean image of 1957. This scene turned mid-show, with special effects, into a mirror image in an all-pink, glamorous version. Our ambition to transform things into something positive was very well executed. On the other hand, we can say that most shows are not satisfactory for us. We are very critical and perfectionist, and most times a show brings about some self-hate and self-doubt. Every time we want to do it better next time, but always it is not perfect. And we find it sometimes torture to see our shows on DVD.

In 2006 Viktor & Rolf followed in the footsteps of their one-time hero, Karl Lagerfeld, and designed a collection for H&M, duly scattered with winsome heart motifs and entitled 'Viktor & Rolf ♡ H&M'. Within minutes the central piece, a wedding dress priced at the none-too-princely sum of £219.99, was selling for ten times that amount on eBay. Overnight the designers, hitherto really known only to the fashion insider, became accessible to the woman – and indeed the man – on the high street. Viktor & Rolf stress, however, that this was a one-off: 'Fashion is elitist. Otherwise it's not luxury. This is something we like as well. H&M was a one-off fun project, and something you can do only once. For us, exhibiting fashion in a museum is a democratic way of showing our work. It's open to everyone, whereas our shows are always for the same small group of about 800 people.'

But, while the audience for their catwalk shows might be small, Viktor & Rolf's audience as a whole is vast, for they – and here, once again, they have always functioned like contemporary artists – are acutely aware of the power of the media. In 2003 the designers celebrated a decade working in fashion with a major exhibition at the Musée de la Mode et du Textile in Paris. The catalogue, called *E-Magazine*, an issue of a fashion magazine published by Artimo, was a collection of press cuttings on the subject of their work gathered over that ten-year period. 'Work exists only when publicized', they argue. That said, however: 'It does not consume us, nor do we depend on it.'

Far more important is the fact that Viktor & Rolf are, as they put it, 'hard-core romantics. We just love the impossible.' Who else working in fashion today would create a wedding dress entirely out of bows? 'Since we come from a couture background, we like bows and ruffles in general. Our "White" collection was made almost entirely out of bows. And the wedding dress we made for Princess Mabel van Oranje-Nassau consisted of 248 bows.' Who else would launch a men's perfume at a show with a live soundtrack (the first to be written for a fragrance) courtesy of Rufus Wainwright, accompanied by eight men ballroom dancing; give up an entire collection to Tilda Swinton; or have Tori Amos playing a grand piano?

opposite:
Long Live the Immaterial (Bluescreen),
Autumn/Winter 2002–03

above:
Advertisement for Viktor & Rolf ♡ H&M, 2006

We admire them deeply. They are authentic spirits, very intelligent and complex beings. Tilda Swinton can go from art house to Hollywood with no problem. Rufus Wainwright can go from camp to deeply emotional in one second. It was quite a shock for us that, even in the fashion world, doing something gay – in this case men dancing – was such an issue. Our fashion is very much an expression of our personality. And it can be idealistic; we see creativity as our weapon to create a more beautiful and interesting world. It was never intended as a political move, but we do like to make a statement, to do something that hasn't been done before. We want to add something to this world, not just to make a nice dress, although this is definitely important. But it's the identity that interests us most.

And so, while it would be all too easy to position Viktor & Rolf as highly sophisticated media manipulators or even agents provocateurs, their viewpoint is, in fact, more heartfelt than that:

We have always regarded fashion and our position within it as a total package, and so any 'branding' came naturally. When we were aspiring to a certain position in fashion – namely, eternal glory – we were instinctively aware of the importance of creating an aura, a magic realm. There was an instant interest in fashion as a whole and not just clothes. We certainly have a lot of doubts and questions regarding fashion, the system, ourselves, but we ultimately always strive to transform any negative feelings into something creative and, hopefully, beautiful. It is our strength to use our emotions, whatever they are, in a creative way and turn them around. 'Flowerbomb' and the recent 'No' show [Autumn/Winter 2008–09] are good examples of that. We love fashion, we are a part of it, but we also think fashion can be much more than we all imagine. By questioning it from within, we try to search for its boundaries, and stretch them, as well as our own.

Cover image for *E-Magazine*, 2003
Photograph: Inez van Lamsweerde and Vinoodh Matadin
Bodypaint: Jos Brands. Hair: Luigi Murenu. Make-up: Peter Philips

COLLECTIONS

HYÈRES
1993

Paris, métro: deformed silhouettes in which you can recognize only some fragments. We used these existing fragments to create a new order. Parts of a suit sewn into a dress, like an archaeologist restoring a Greek vase. A dress existing of layers of shirts; the longing to hide. … A deformation accomplished by linings much bigger than the garments they belong to, which are far too small. Cut of sequins to show the beauty of decay. Like an archaeologist who finds a remaining piece of history. A collection as a testimony.
(*Purple Prose*, no. 4, Autumn 1993)

On graduating from the Arnhem Academy of Art and Design in 1992, when they were still in their early twenties, Viktor & Rolf moved to Paris to launch a career in fashion design. Their first collection was designed and made in a tiny apartment, and literally filled the entire space. They later explained that the collection's extreme silhouettes and multiple layers, which concealed and disfigured the wearer's body, were an expression of the alienation they experienced in Paris; they felt dwarfed by the city, and longed to hide themselves from it.

Exploring ideas of distortion and layering, these first experimental pieces won Viktor & Rolf the top three prizes at the prestigious fashion competition the Salon Européen des Jeunes Stylistes, at Hyères in southern France.

Soon after the competition, a 'destroyed' dress with short jacket made it on to the cover of the cult French fashion–art–literature crossover magazine *Purple Prose*, while the rest of the collection was illustrated inside under the title 'Détachement'. Stacked collars, which would be examined more fully later in the designers' career, made their first appearance here, on an oversized coat with three collars.

Most of the pieces from the collection have since been lost, although one ensemble (opposite) was purchased by the Centraal Museum, Utrecht, in 2000.

Viktor & Rolf realized their first installation as part of the group show *L'Hiver de l'Amour* (*The Winter of Love*) at the Musée d'Art Moderne de la Ville de Paris, curated by Elein Fleiss and Olivier Zahm of *Purple Prose*, along with the artists Dominique Gonzalez-Foerster, Bernard Joisten and Jean-Luc Vilmouth. The installation contained pieces from their second collection, of March 1994, which the designers also had photographed worn by a model. It signalled Viktor & Rolf's pioneering departure from the distressed aesthetic associated with deconstruction in fashion. Loosely based on historical costumes from such periods as the French Second Empire, headless figures entrapped behind glass, wearing voluminous coats and dresses fashioned in PVC, announced a look that managed to be both formally restrained and surreal.

Importantly for their future success, *L'Hiver de l'Amour* brought Viktor & Rolf into contact with fellow exhibition contributor Inez van Lamsweerde, who together with Vinoodh Matadin became a rising star of the fashion-photography world. The exhibition travelled to the public art space P.S.1 in New York, bringing the designers highly desirable exposure in the United States.

above:
Installation on the occasion of the re-opening of the Centraal Museum,
Utrecht, The Netherlands, November 1999–February 2000

In the mid-1990s Viktor & Rolf felt that the world embraced fashion's ephemera – the supermodel, the designer as star – rather than dealt with what fashion is about: cloth and form. They decided to explore what they saw as a troubling emergence of emptiness, and took as a starting point the superficiality of gift-wrapping decorations and bonbon boxes.

The designers realized this collection in an installation for which they hired Galerie Patricia Dorfmann, Paris. The installation comprised five different golden silhouettes suspended from the ceiling, each casting a 'shadow' on the floor: a flat, black, wearable garment in organza. The lamé garments were inspired by luxurious gift wrapping, and featured elements reminiscent of trailing ribbons, enveloping nothing but air. Viktor & Rolf intended to evoke the overblown elegance of fashion and its deflated flipside. On the wall they listed the world's top models in gold vinyl, and in the background played a recording of schoolchildren reciting these names, as if learning the alphabet.

L'Apparence du Vide (*The Appearance of the Void*) signalled the first of a number of references in the work of Viktor & Rolf to the immaterial and colour-saturated empire of Yves Klein. Here, Viktor & Rolf knowingly recalled Klein's notorious installation *Le Vide* (*The Void*) of 1958, and his gold monochrome paintings of the early 1960s. In a similar fashion to Klein, who staked all on the high wire straddled between celebrity and spectacle on the one hand and transcendence and pure sensibility on the other, Viktor & Rolf's 'gold' collection pinpointed the vacuous and commercially driven nature of the fashion world while simultaneously celebrating it.

The installation was enthusiastically received, being reviewed by *Purple Prose* editor Olivier Zahm for the respected contemporary art magazine *Artforum* in December 1995, and making it on to the pages of the influential fashion magazine *Visionaire* (no. 17), in a feature that included a model seemingly suspended in mid-air, photographed by Viktor & Rolf.

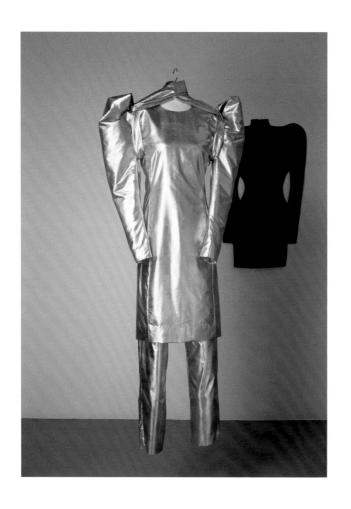

bridget
carla
cindy
claudia
elle
eva
helena
karen
kate
kristen
linda
meghan
michelle
nadja
naomi
niki
shalom
stella
stephanie
tatjana
trish
yasmeen

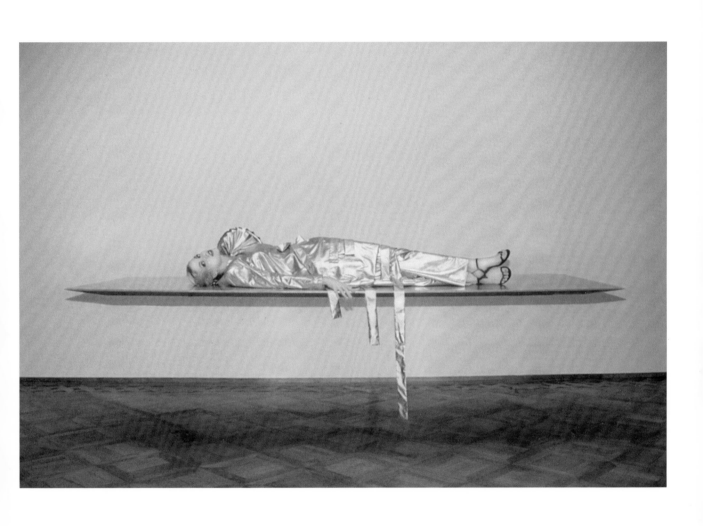

"Viktor & Rolf on strike/en grève, winter/hiver '96/'97"

VIKTOR & ROLF ON STRIKE
AUTUMN/WINTER 1996–97

Struggling to realize and stage a collection for every season, as the fashion industry dictates, and equally frustrated by a lack of exposure in the press, Viktor & Rolf took to the streets with an audacious show of self-promotion. Posters announcing 'Viktor & Rolf on strike' were sent to magazine editors as well as being plastered across Paris during fashion week in March 1996. Although the poster may not have received much media attention at the time, adopting alternative strategies in this way allowed the designers to secure further their cutting-edge credentials while hinting at their future prominent place in the media.

opposite:
'On strike' doll, 2008

LAUNCH
1996

From the beginning, Viktor & Rolf have sought to comment on the world of fashion as commodity and excess, while at the same time aspiring to be successful – highly successful – within it. There can be no doubt that they love fashion, its history and its forms. The installation *Launch* at the Torch Gallery in Amsterdam encapsulated all their aspirations for the future. Viktor & Rolf were impatient with their situation as fledgling artists and could not wait to fulfil their childhood dreams. Their vision of a design studio, catwalk show, photo shoot and boutique was realized in miniature. Perfume being the ultimate symbol of a fashion house's success, the installation also included a life-size stand for Le Parfum – a fictitious perfume that Viktor & Rolf produced in a limited edition of 250 bottles that were sealed shut. The perfume was accompanied by a real publicity still, the concept of which was developed by Viktor & Rolf; it was photographed by Wendelien Daan and published in V magazine in the autumn of 1996 and in *Blvd* in 1997.

Viktor & Rolf later commented that the scent's intoxicating effect, anticipated by its publicity image, could only ever be imagined: sealed by a wax cap, the flask could not be opened. The perfume could neither evaporate nor give off its scent, and would forever be a potential, a pure promise. This conceptual bravado was reminiscent of such seminal artworks as Marcel Duchamp's bottled *Air de Paris* (1919), Yves Klein's sale of space in return for pure gold (*Zones of Immaterial Pictorial Sensibility*, 1960) and Piero Manzoni's canned *Artist's Shit* (1961).

In 2004, with the launch of the usable fragrance Flowerbomb, and in 2005, with the opening of their boutique in Milan, Viktor & Rolf realized the dream that was *Launch*.

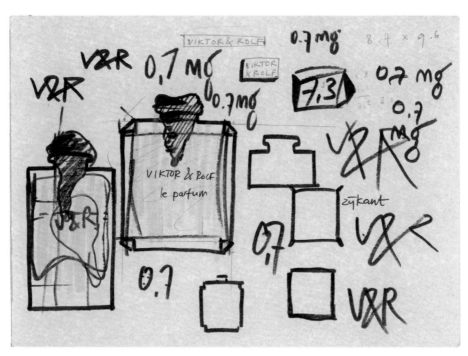

above:
Le Parfum, 1996
Photograph: Wendelien Daan
Published in V, no. 7, Fall 1996

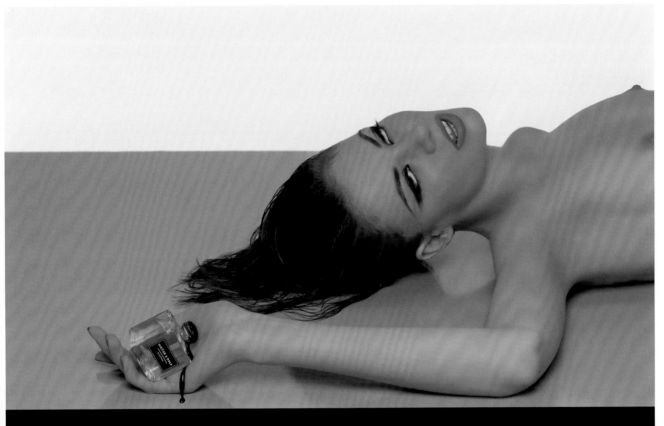

Le Parfum publicity still, 1996
Photograph: Wendelien Daan
Published in *Blvd*, Winter 1997

FIRST COUTURE COLLECTION
SPRING/SUMMER 1998

Viktor & Rolf have compared haute couture to a laboratory in which they can freely experiment with ideas, and in 1998, after five years on the margins, they were finally able to present their first-ever couture collection on a catwalk to an eager audience of prospective buyers and press. This momentous occasion inspired the designers to present a show in which each outfit was a study in the different elements that make up a couture garment: fabric, colour, embroidery, accessory and ornament. For instance, a coat dress, later photographed by Inez van Lamsweerde and Vinoodh Matadin (opposite), was emblazoned with multiple circle-shaped embroideries, one of which was left unfinished to show the process of the craft of embroidery. Isolated and privileged in this way, the various elements could be used to create entirely unorthodox and often highly sculptural forms that also celebrated the craftsmanship of couture.

The show also provided Viktor & Rolf with the means to explore performance in a way that had hitherto been unavailable to them. Elegiac and monolithic, it began with each model standing motionless on a plinth, reflecting the collection's central concept of putting couture on a pedestal. A soundtrack had the name 'Viktor & Rolf' repeated by different voices, mantra-like. One show-stopping ensemble was a white silk dress with voluminous collar, worn with a white boater and an oversized pearl necklace. The model threw first the hat then the necklace to the floor, where they shattered, revealing themselves to be made of porcelain. As Viktor & Rolf have stated, this gesture was a comment on the disproportionate value given to accessories within the fashion industry.

Photograph: Inez van Lamsweerde and Vinoodh Matadin
Styling: Franciscus Ankoné
Published in *New York Times Magazine*, March 1998

Missy, 1997
Photograph: Inez van Lamsweerde and Vinoodh Matadin
Styling: Viktor & Rolf. Hair: Eugene Souleiman. Make-up: Lisa Butler
Published in *Vogue Deutsch*, December 1997

Photograph: Anuschka Blommers and Niels Schumm
Styling: Suzanne Koller
Published in *Self Service*, no. 8, Summer 1998

ATOMIC BOMB
AUTUMN/WINTER 1998–99

Towards the end of the 1990s, thoughts turned to the next millennium and what it would bring. Viktor & Rolf's collection for Autumn/Winter 1998–99 concerned itself with two possible scenarios: 'We were wondering if Nostradamus was going to be right and the world would be coming to its end, or if it was going to be the biggest party ever' (SHOWstudio.com).

Viktor & Rolf's audacious answer was to make a collection around the silhouette of the mushroom cloud produced by an atomic bomb. They used silk padding to inflate the clothes, and further elaborated the theme with tinsel, streamers, balloons and pompoms. This magisterial state of eruption, displayed to the soundtrack of a reworking of Prince's '1999', was followed by Viktor & Rolf's so-called 'anti-climax': models parading in the same outfits but this time with the stuffing removed (see 'Balloons', p. 66). The show, portentously programmed between Chanel and Christian Lacroix, was highly acclaimed, not only for its surreal theatricality but also for the way in which the clothes gracefully draped and fell around the body once their gargantuan implants were removed.

While welcoming the new millennium, 'Atomic Bomb' also saluted the twentieth century. Viktor & Rolf incorporated vintage fabrics by Chanel, Balenciaga and Pucci, sourced from the Parisian manufacturer René Véron, and the collection also had echoes of Rei Kawakubo's notorious 'Dress Meets Body, Body Meets Dress' collection of Spring/Summer 1997, where the clothes had built-in bumps. Collaborators Inez van Lamsweerde and Vinoodh Matadin helped cast and style the show, while also utilizing the collection for various shoots, including one that appeared in *The Independent Magazine* in October 1998. Philip Treacy designed the hats.

'Harlequin' doll, 2008

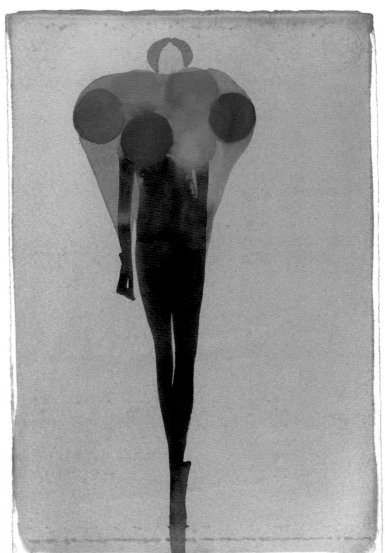

above, right:
Illustration: Mats Gustafson
Published in *Visionaire's Fashion 2001*, 1999

opposite:
'Balloons' doll, 2008

68

Photograph: Anuschka Blommers and Niels Schumm
Styling: Suzanne Koller
Published in *Self Service*, no. 9, Fall 1998

opposite:
Photograph: Bettina Komenda
Styling: Karl Plewka
Published in *Interview*, November 1998

above and pages 76 and 77:
Photographs: Inez van Lamsweerde and Vinoodh Matadin
Styling: Nancy Rohde. Hair: Eugene Souleiman. Make-up: Lisa Butler
Published in *Visionaire*, no. 25, July 1998

BLACK LIGHT
SPRING/SUMMER 1999

The ideas that underpin Viktor & Rolf's output can, in most cases, be read as autobiographical in essence. The designers described the 'Black Light' collection as a reflection of the feeling they had at the time that things were working out. Their sense of victory was translated into a black-and-white show, the first part of which was shown in black light, the second in white – as if they had conquered their demons and were in the spotlight.

Signature Viktor & Rolf tropes – the ironic and yet celebratory commentary on fashion itself, tailoring, the play on oversized elements, the carefully choreographed use of colour, texture and form – were now joined by the deployment of striking formal opposites. Black and white were used to startling effect, as was the contrast between masculine and feminine forms. The collection utilized classic evening-wear items – the tuxedo, the little black dress and the tailored shirt – all made in one elegant fabric: silk gazar. When the collection was first shown in black ultraviolet light, only white details were illuminated, exposing the detailing; for instance, a huge all-ruffle shirt or plastic tubes arranged like a skeleton. In some cases only an outline was seen by the audience, rather than something that could be perceived as a garment. After being shown once, the collection was shown again, this time with the black light switched to white, and only then were the full ensembles seen.

KO1
han
ne
lore

sh
39
sch!

lisa as models
sh. 39

K10
schmidt

IIII

k13
sh 40

silvia 'mg'

k
KO4
Jelena

K 13
silvia
sh
40

LANG

KO6
kistler

sch!

KO7
skelet
linda
41

Lola
click

kog

KO5
lisa

K 14

ludmilla
nero sh. 40

Photograph: Inez van Lamsweerde and Vinoodh Matadin
Styling: Viktor & Rolf
Published in *Visionaire's Fashion 2001*, 1999

Photograph: Anuschka Blommers and Niels Schumm
Styling: Karl Plewka
Published in *Interview*, May 1999

Photograph: Markus Jans
Styling: Isabelle Peyrut
Published in *Libération Supplément*, 10 March 1999

With their next couture collection, Viktor & Rolf created arguably their most memorable and truly original show up to that point. Eschewing the catwalk convention of a procession in which each model wears one outfit, the show featured one model who wore the entire collection – at once. Furthermore, she was dressed live by the designers themselves. The model, Maggie Rizer, arrived on stage wearing the first garment, a short dress made of coarsely woven jute and silk satin, and stepped into a pair of shoes on a turntable, rotating like a figurine in a music box. She was then slowly dressed in eight additional layers of couture dresses, each heavily embroidered with crystals and lace, and each referred to by the designers as a 'preparation' for the next layer. The preparations acted as pieces in a puzzle, each new layer completing or mirroring a detail or an element on the preceding tier. For example, a bow on the hem of the second preparation was both concealed and echoed by a sash on the hem of the third preparation. Once each layer was in place, the turntable revolved and the designers brought in the next preparation, creating a Russian doll in reverse. The preparations were made predominantly of jute, which is among the most affordable natural textiles, and traditionally used for packaging goods. The result of using jute in a collection dedicated to exclusivity was a striking contrast of opposites – a theme that was slowly emerging as a signature motif in the work of Viktor & Rolf.

RUSSIAN DOLL
AUTUMN/WINTER 1999–2000

The show was staged in a small space with only 125 invited guests, and Viktor & Rolf commented that the collection was a paean to the exclusivity and unavailability of fashion. In an interview for *i-D* magazine, they compared the act of lavishing attention on Rizer to worshipping an icon or goddess. Writing in the same magazine in May 2000, a witness to the event, Jamie Huckbody, described the final stages of the performance, which eventually saw the model wearing more than 70 kilograms (150 lb) of exquisite haute couture: 'Finally she was honoured with a garland of white flowers at her feet and draped in outfit number ten [the sixth preparation was made of two layers], a simple cape that cocooned her bloated frame and crowned her shoulder with a gigantic over-blown rose. Chrysalis, alien, empress, model in a linen body bag, whatever. Ideas like this defy description and are hard to live up to' (*i-D*, no. 197, May 2000, p. 104).

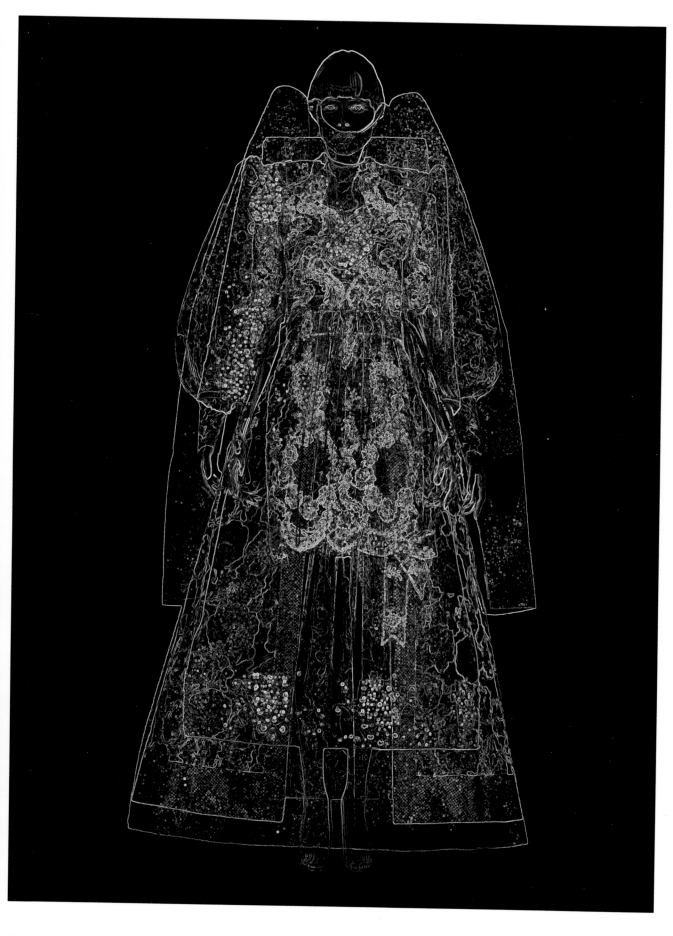

Illustration: François Berthoud
Published in *Dazed & Confused*, no. 87, March 2002

page 90:
'First preparation' doll, 2008

page 91:
'Fourth and fifth preparations' doll, 2008

above:
Photograph: Bardo Fabiani
Realization: Anna Piaggi
Published in *Vogue Italia*, 'Alta Moda' supplement, September 1999

opposite:
'Final preparation' doll, 2008

We want to be powerful in our own way.
(Viktor & Rolf, *The Observer Magazine*, 21 May 2000)

Until this time, couture had been Viktor & Rolf's laboratory for experiment, but, as high fashion is an exclusive sphere and receives little attention even in the fashion media, it was not bringing them the global success they were unashamedly seeking. For their first ready-to-wear collection, entitled 'Stars & Stripes', the designers took inspiration from the American flag. Viktor & Rolf, with a knowing irony, melded their own desire for fashion domination with the spread of American culture and values across the globe: 'We used American icons as a metaphor for our own desire to become a big global brand' (SHOWstudio.com). The signature ensemble, a Stars-and-Stripes-emblazoned trouser suit, shirt and coat, was worn by the supermodel Alek Wek in a shoot for the *New York Times Magazine*'s 'Fashions of the Times' issue in the autumn of 2000. The collection reconsidered such stock clothing types as the tailored suit, the smoking jacket, the pinstripe shirt and American jeans – twinned with Viktor & Rolf's signature ruffle shirt. Furthermore, as the designers have said about some of the garments: 'We started wrapping up the outfits in black fabric so that some were partially, and others were totally, wrapped ... by wrapping something up we make it more personal' (*i-D*, no. 197, May 2000).

An instant commercial success, 'Stars & Stripes' was stocked by the likes of Barneys and Jeffrey in New York, Liberty, Joseph and The Pineal Eye in London, and Colette in Paris. Unlike Viktor & Rolf's couture collections, it was indeed, as Tamsin Blanchard pointed out, 'cheap, wearable, and washable' (*The Observer Magazine*, 21 May 2000).

It was at this time that Viktor & Rolf launched their logo, a wax seal bearing the monogram 'V&R', which, as logos often do, made the brand more visible and has since become central to their commercial success. They later commented: 'It's like a stamp of approval' (SHOWstudio.com). Viktor & Rolf were now truly a brand in their own right.

opposite and pages 100 and 101:
'Look book' images
Photographs: Anuschka Blommers and Niels Schumm
Styling: Viktor & Rolf

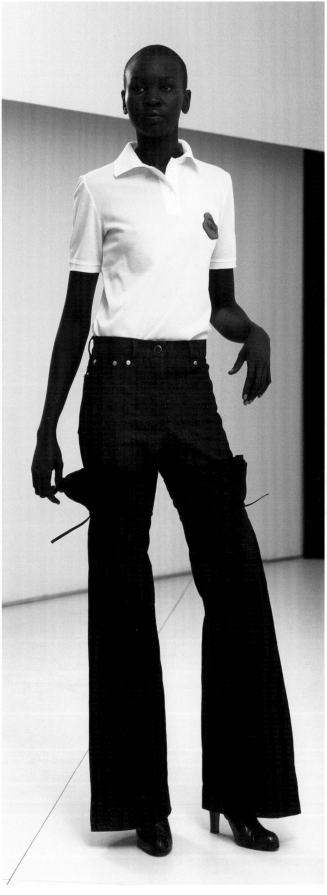

carmen

ann catherine

Jade

BELLS
AUTUMN/WINTER 2000–01

Viktor & Rolf's fifth haute couture catwalk collection was an extraordinary multi-sensory experience. Garments were heavily embroidered with brass bells that, when worn, created a shimmering, sonorous effect of great elegance and mystery. The show was carefully choreographed to ensure that the eagerly waiting audience heard the garments before they emerged from shrouds of fog, visible for a brief moment before passing again into the mist. For Viktor & Rolf, the show was about creating an aura, grasping the intangible. One defining ensemble comprised a full-length dress of green silk crêpe georgette and an enormous coat fully covered with bells of various sizes. In some cases the bells worked to emphasize either the function or an element of a garment. For example, the classic satin piping on smoking trousers was covered with bells, while the draped neckline of a little black cocktail dress was partly created by the weight of the bells on a decorative rose at the midriff. The asymmetry of dresses was fashioned by bell belts hanging on one side.

Since it was the year 2000, Viktor & Rolf invited *Generation X* author Douglas Coupland to write the programme, which included a short essay entitled 'The Glittering Rubble'. Coupland also gave the garments titles, which, as he noted in the *New York Times* on 8 August 2006, were 'composites formed from names of early 1950s Nevada nuclear test-drops of atomic bombs, random snatches of life in the digital world and three-letter acronyms germane to the modern world'.

page 103:
'WWWXXX "Dawn" Would You Like Another Transaction? World Wide Web Pornography' doll, 2008

above:
Photograph: Gérard Uféras
Published in *The Fashion*, no. 1, Autumn/Winter 2000–01

Photograph: David Sims
Fashion editor: Michel Botbol
Published in *Harper's Bazaar*, October 2000

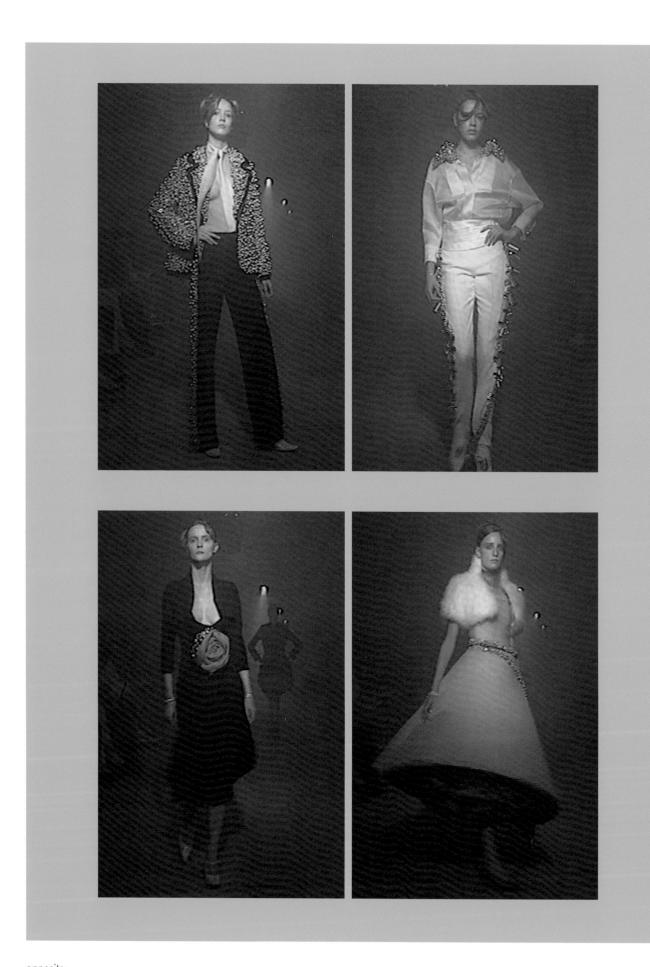

opposite:
'CIA DMZ "WASP" YOU'VE GOT MAIL Central Intelligence Agency Demilitarized Zone' doll, 2008

SKIRT: VDC104A VC00bD
PANT: VDC200A VC00uA

SHIRT: VDC308A VC00u

34

PRESS
1
MINI

DEVON

38

SPECIAL.

NNA

10

Devon
SPECIAL

10.

DEVON

BLACK HOLE
AUTUMN/WINTER 2001–02

In this collection the mood of Viktor & Rolf's work was one of ominous foreboding. 'Inspired by a shadow', funereal and sinister, the 'Black Hole' collection was entirely black (*Self Service*, no. 15, Fall/Winter 2001, p. 153). On the catwalk, even the models were given blacked-out faces. The silhouette was given prominence over everything else, with subtleties carefully crafted in the varying textures and tailoring.

Viktor & Rolf have commented that the collection came out of their own depression and was a way of making empty shapes visible. In fact, dealing with their state of mind through a creative process produced one of the most acclaimed collections in the designers' career. The exclusion of all pattern and colour from the collection allowed the duo to concentrate on the elements of silhouette and texture. Using a variety of fabrics and materials, including different mixes of silk as well as lurex, felt and bouclé, Viktor & Rolf played with such classic shapes as the bell skirt, the two-piece, the shirt dress, the Victorian dress, the little black dress and the tuxedo. Alongside one-off pieces they showed sharply cut ready-to-wear garments, and it is the marriage of the two that was responsible for the critical and commercial success of the collection.

page 114:
'Devon' doll, 2008

113

above:
Photograph: Arthur Elgort
Fashion editor: Grace Coddington
Published in American *Vogue*, June 2001

opposite:
Illustration: François Berthoud, 2001

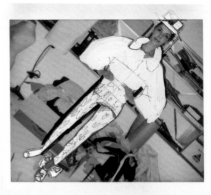

WHITE
SPRING/SUMMER 2002

Following the dark mood of the previous season, and reflecting its huge success, Viktor & Rolf's next collection was imbued with a feeling of optimism and romance. The all-white garments carried a profusion of bows, ribbons and volume. Previously used Viktor & Rolf motifs, such as the oversized and the multiple, were reintroduced: for example, a shirt with five bow collars, or three layers of trousers integrated to make one piece. The show was held at Maison de Radio France, and its famous pipe organ was used alongside a pre-

recorded mix by the Dutch DJ Eddy De Clercq, a regular collaborator of the designers. Love hearts appeared on huge charm bracelets and charm necklaces (made by the designers Studio Job), which were worn as chains.

The following year Her Royal Highness Princess Mabel van Oranje-Nassau commissioned the designers to make her wedding dress, a duchesse satin gown adorned with 248 bows and trailing a 3-metre (9-ft 10-in.) train. Increasing in size to gigantic proportions, the bows represented a lover's knot.

Her Royal Highness Princess Mabel van Oranje-Nassau
on her wedding day, 24 April 2004

Illustration: Mats Gustafson
Published in *Vogue Italia*, January 2002

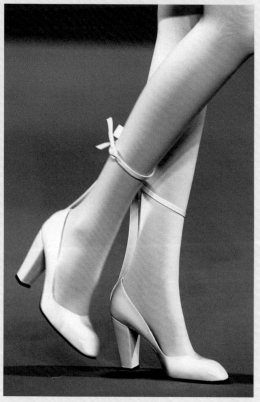

details of the garments were transformed by a technological process: in this case, the incorporation of sections of chromakey blue. These sections came to life on giant screens on either side of the stage, the blue replaced by breathtaking footage from the natural and urban worlds. The cut and detail of the clothes were inspired by army and naval themes, including variations on pea coats, rope designs and a multitude of pockets and compartments. A large paisley print was a central graphic motif. Seen on screen, the models seemed to be wearing the imagery, almost becoming cityscapes, snow-clad mountains, sphinxes, birds soaring, divers plunging, highways, kaleidoscopic coral reefs and open seas. The collection was a meditation on both the fleeting nature of fashion and the ability of the imagination to surpass matter. At the same time, the show also provided strong evidence of the extent to which Viktor & Rolf are aware of and in thrall to the power of the image.

Borrowing its title from Yves Klein's famous exclamation, this collection reflected Viktor & Rolf's desire to 'go beyond the product, to design something that is immaterial' (SHOWstudio.com). To communicate their ideas about the ephemeral nature of fashion, the designers adapted 'bluescreen' technology, used in the film and television industry to create special effects through the juxtaposition and overlapping of separate images. As with the 'Black Light' collection, certain

pages 126 and 127 and above:
Photographs: Anuschka Blommers and Niels Schumm
Styling: Viktor & Rolf
Published in *Interview*, December 2002/January 2003

Having recently received an invitation from L'Oréal to create their first perfume, Viktor & Rolf had immersed themselves in the world of scent when they conceived this flower-themed collection. Guests at the fashion show found a bottle of rose essence on their seats, hinting at the designers' new venture as well as at what was about to unfold on the catwalk.

Dancing and twirling as if intoxicated by a powerful scent, the models wore a dazzling array of highly feminine and colourful garments, with a predominance of chiffon and floral prints. The collection featured such outfits as full-length tiered dresses, sometimes with multiple patterns. Two signature pieces, a dress and a coat, were both meticulously hand-stitched with hundreds of multicoloured silk flowers. The garments were complemented by Afro hairdos, plaits and brightly coloured hairpieces, as well as vintage jewellery of floral and ribbon motifs by the French house of Van Cleef & Arpels.

Photograph: Inez van Lamsweerde and Vinoodh Matadin
Styling: Alex White
Published in W, April 2003

Photographs: Anuschka Blommers and Niels Schumm
Styling: Viktor & Rolf
Published in *Vogue Nippon*, June 2003

Photograph: Herb Ritts
Fashion editor: Tonne Goodman
Published in American *Vogue*, February 2003

Photograph: Juergen Teller
Styling: Joe Zee
Published in W, December 2002

Photograph: Walter Chin
Styling: Susanne Kölmel
Published in *Vogue Deutsch*, January 2003

ERIN O

RAQUEL

38

3

36

25

ONE WOMAN SHOW
AUTUMN/WINTER 2003–04

A chance meeting with Tilda Swinton attending the 'Russian Doll' collection was followed by her approach to Viktor & Rolf to dress her for the Golden Globe Awards ceremony in 2001. A deep friendship developed, as well as more commissions, culminating in one of the most fruitful collaborations in Viktor & Rolf's career to date – a collection dedicated to Swinton. Reluctant to call the actress their muse, the designers have said: 'The romantic use of the term "muse" may carry connotations of passivity, but ours has played an active part in our creative process' (SHOWstudio.com).

Taking inspiration to its positive extreme, the duo invited Swinton to write and recite a tone poem at their show. A manifesto to individuality, the poem concluded with the words: 'There is only one of you. Only one.' All the models were made to look like Swinton, who modelled on the catwalk too.

At the ten-year anniversary of their collaboration, the designers turned to themes of volume, stacking and distortion. The collection was designed to apply their, by now, signature looks to a wearable modern-day wardrobe for a woman, in this case Swinton. The actress confirmed that 'Viktor & Rolf made a collection of clothes that I wear every day' (SHOWstudio.com). The anniversary was also marked, later that year, by a solo exhibition at the Musée de la Mode et du Textile, Paris, the first since Yves Saint Laurent's in 1986.

opposite:
'Simone' doll, 2008

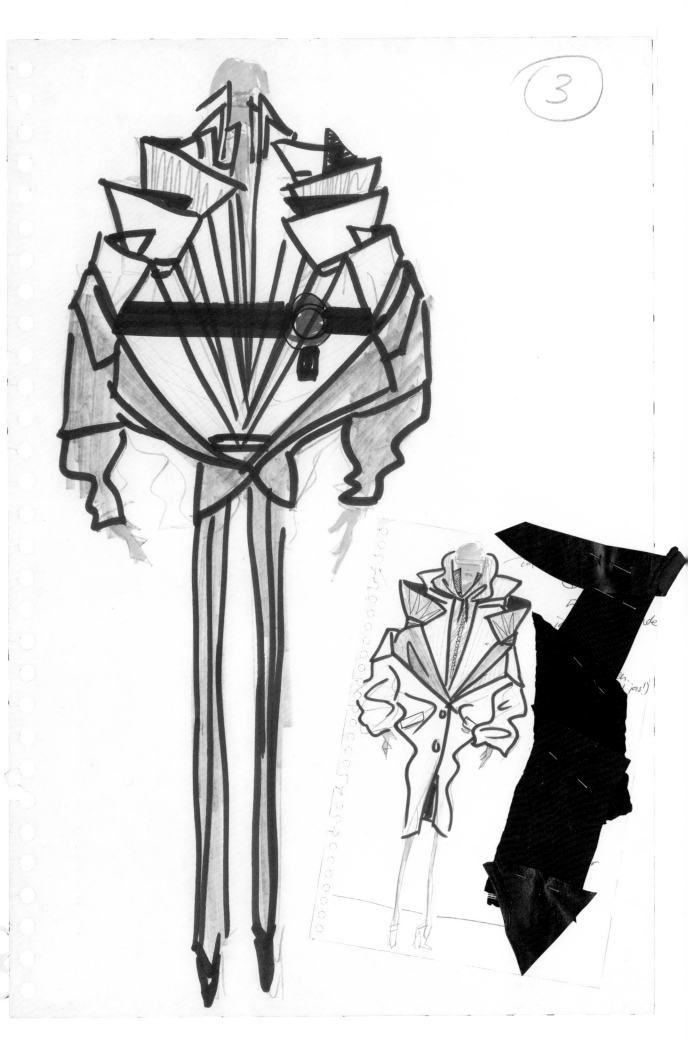

Photographs: Inez van Lamsweerde and Vinoodh Matadin
Fashion editor: Brana Wolf
Published in *Harper's Bazaar*, October 2003

THE RED SHOES
SPRING/SUMMER 2004

The exploration of opposites has been a staple of Viktor & Rolf's idiom from the beginning of their creative partnership: light and dark, the real and the intangible, the exclusive and the global. Here the designers' experiments with feminine and masculine silhouettes produced a new equation that juxtaposed iconic pieces for both genders: the evening gown and the smoking jacket. For example, several of the outfits contrasted delicate dresses of silk and tulle with trousers. As in previous collections, Viktor & Rolf's signature tuxedo was present. In one version the jacket with tails was cut off the shoulder and hung by straps like a camisole.

A parallel theme of fantasy and old Hollywood glamour was consolidated by a soundtrack of such musical hits as 'Somewhere Over the Rainbow'. Each outfit was twinned with a different pair of red shoes: stilettos in glitter or leather, slingbacked or open-toed, evoking some of the most memorable imagery in cinema history from such films as *The Wizard of Oz* (1939) and Michael Powell and Emeric Pressburger's *The Red Shoes* (1948).

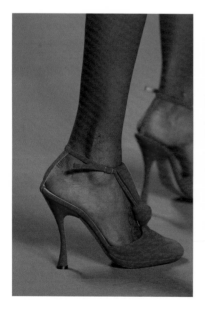

Photograph: Lee Broomfield
Published in British *Vogue*, March 2004

opposite:
'Mariacarla' doll, 2008

FLOWERBOMB
SPRING/SUMMER 2005

A show of extravagance and extremes, 'Flowerbomb' was one of the most important moments in Viktor & Rolf's career. It opened with a heavy rock soundtrack, to which the models strode down the catwalk wearing a variety of entirely black clothes, from simple leather jackets to a full-scale ribbon rosette engulfing its wearer, each outfit completed by a blacked-out motorcycle helmet. Bows and ribbons were a central motif, increasing in size from one outfit to the next. The show seemed to close when the models arranged themselves as if frozen into a *tableau vivant* based on the famous photograph by Loomis Dean of Christian Dior models from 1957. But, with a countdown and a pyrotechnic display, the stage revolved to reveal a positive mirror image of the same tableau in numerous shades of pink and gold, each outfit an open bouquet of ribbons or bows, like an exquisite partly unwrapped luxury gift. And each of these pink-and-gold confections was a counterpart to one of the black outfits, as if the explosion had launched the models into the designers' concept of a 'flowerbombed' world of positivism.

In addition, the show marked the launch of Viktor & Rolf's first (real) perfume, also called Flowerbomb. The duo had set themselves the task of learning about every aspect of perfume production, visiting Grasse, France's fragrance capital, to familiarize themselves with the basics of scent creation. The result has been a huge international success.

page 156:
'Sena' doll, 2008

page 157:
'Karolina' doll, 2008

colour.

23.

48

Flowerbomb publicity still, 2004
Photograph: Inez van Lamsweerde and Vinoodh Matadin

BEDTIME STORY
AUTUMN/WINTER 2005–06

This bedroom-themed collection was Viktor & Rolf's move to a more intimate and private sensibility, following the effervescent 'Flowerbomb' show. In this show, singer–songwriter Tori Amos performed at a grand piano, playing a specially written soundtrack that complemented the dreamy atmosphere and was inspired by the biblical love poem Song of Solomon. The garments were abundant with details inspired by bedclothes: broderie anglaise, quilting and ruffles. Bedsheets became sumptuous, cascading gowns; duvets became quilted coats and smoking jackets; satin pillows became gargantuan collar supports that framed the face. The single red rose was a central motif, as were the words 'I love you'.

opposite:
'Raquel' doll, 2008

164

166

above, left:
Illustration: Mats Gustafson, 2005

page 170:
'Hana' doll, 2008

page 171:
'Tiiu' doll, 2008

In April 2005 Viktor & Rolf opened their Milan boutique, an exquisite Neo-classical interior in which the furniture and fittings hang upside down. In October of the same year the duo presented their similarly topsy-turvy vision for the next Spring/Summer season. The 'Upside Down' collection showcased couture pieces that could be worn bottom up or bottom down; on the catwalk they were presented first one way and then the other. Applying the same absurd logic, the collection was also presented in reverse, opening with what would normally be the finale: the appearance of Viktor & Rolf. Guests were then treated to the procession that signals the conclusion of the show and after that the presentation of the signature 'final' look. The visual conceit was carried through to the last detail: the backdrop bore Viktor & Rolf's logo, flanked on either side by a huge bouquet of flowers bursting from a vase on a tall plinth – all faultlessly displayed upside down. Diana Ross's song 'Upside Down' was played in reverse as accompaniment. The collection was characterized by flowing shapes contrasted with masculine tailoring. Couture dresses had soft silhouettes and long hemlines; bib collars were sewn askew and coats fastened asymmetrically.

UPSIDE DOWN
SPRING/SUMMER 2006

Photograph: Mario Sorrenti
Styling: Andrew Richardson
Published in V, no. 39, Spring 2006

SILVER
AUTUMN/WINTER 2006–07

Drawing on the Dutch tradition of silver-plating a baby's first shoe as a keepsake, the 'Silver' collection once again featured classic clothing forms, this time partially plated in silver. It was clearly a metaphor for a desire to give permanence to fashion and still its fleeting nature. A throwback to the catwalk shows of the 1950s, the collection was staged in a dramatic semi-darkened space with three large pools of light in which the models stopped and posed. Similarly inspired dresses were complemented by fishnet stockings and lattice face masks reminiscent of couture veils. The final look was a strapless wedding dress with a wide, petticoated, knee-length skirt, all silver-plated, including the bride's bouquet.

In 2007 Viktor & Rolf were invited by curator Judith King to contribute to an exhibition of site-specific installations at Belsay Hall in Northumberland, a historic house designed by Sir Charles Monck in 1807. Held in trust by English Heritage, the house has, since 1996, provided the context for a series of group projects by an eclectic mix of artists and designers. Viktor & Rolf proposed a silvered bride to grace Monck's beautifully proportioned Greek Revival 'pillar hall'. Reminiscent of their first couture collection, where models stood on sculptural plinths, their bride for Belsay, a goddess literally dripping in silver, represented an ode to fashion itself.

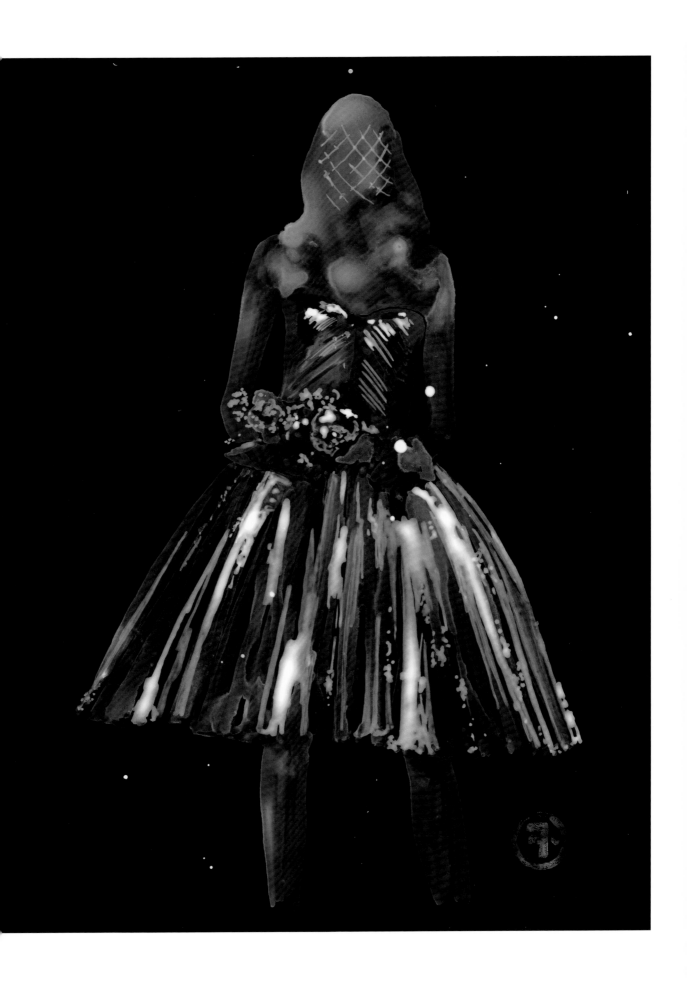

Illustration: François Berthoud, 2006

agressive
romantic
realism

black dress
white shirt
french coat
cocktail dress
evening

opposite:
'Solange' doll, 2008

182

Installation shots from *Picture House*, Belsay Hall,
Northumberland, 2007

'Caroline' doll, 2008

BALLROOM
SPRING/SUMMER 2007

Viktor & Rolf have said of the 'Ballroom' collection: 'We were in the mood to do something entertaining, and we love the fact that ballroom dancing looks very easy and very frivolous but at the same time it's very complicated and about control. We wanted to use the frivolous elements of ballroom like fringes and nude Lycra but to use them in a very strict and classic way' (vogue.com).

Celebrating the traditional clothing forms to be found on the ballroom dance floor, the collection featured skin-coloured Lycra heavily embroidered with Swarovski crystal droplets, star motifs and a profusion of flounces and frills peeping out from the hemlines of jackets.

The collection was also a showcase for the launch of the first male fragrance from the Viktor & Rolf brand, which the designers named Antidote. Singer–songwriter Rufus Wainwright performed a live set throughout the show, and, at the moment of the perfume's unveiling, a group of male dancers in tails danced in couples while Wainwright sang a track composed especially for the fragrance.

Photograph: Jan Welters
Styling: Paola Artioli
Published in *D, la Repubblica delle donne*, April 2007

THE FASHION SHOW
AUTUMN/WINTER 2007–08

Viktor & Rolf took the idea of the fashion show and its accoutrements as the conceptual starting point for this collection. They 'wanted to emphasize how important the idea of the fashion show is to us – so each outfit is a self-sufficient fashion show' (chinadaily.com.cn). For the catwalk show itself, each model was dressed as a walking event, 'a microcosm' of Viktor & Rolf, harnessed to independent lighting and sound systems suspended from their very own scaffolding rigs (chinadaily.com.cn). Privileging the silhouette, the rigging became like an extension of the body, allowing the voluminous forms – a mainstay of the Viktor & Rolf label – to be variously suspended, draped and gathered.

Each of the pieces was characterized by the stylistic tropes of Dutch traditional costume, in particular the clog-wearing Dutch maiden carrying a yoke with two pails of milk. Viktor & Rolf used richly textured fabrics with checks and floral patterns well known in The Netherlands, adorned by ribbons hand-painted by the only artisans to keep this tradition alive. Models wore a modern variation of the familiar coral dog-collar necklace, not closed with the usual large ornamental silver or gold clasp, but with the Viktor & Rolf seal. The collection also featured a pleat technique that is derived from the way that garments are traditionally starched and folded in cupboards. The Staphorst-style and Delft blue clogs, all hand-painted, had heels and were emblazoned with a V&R seal.

opposite:
'Maryna' doll, 2008

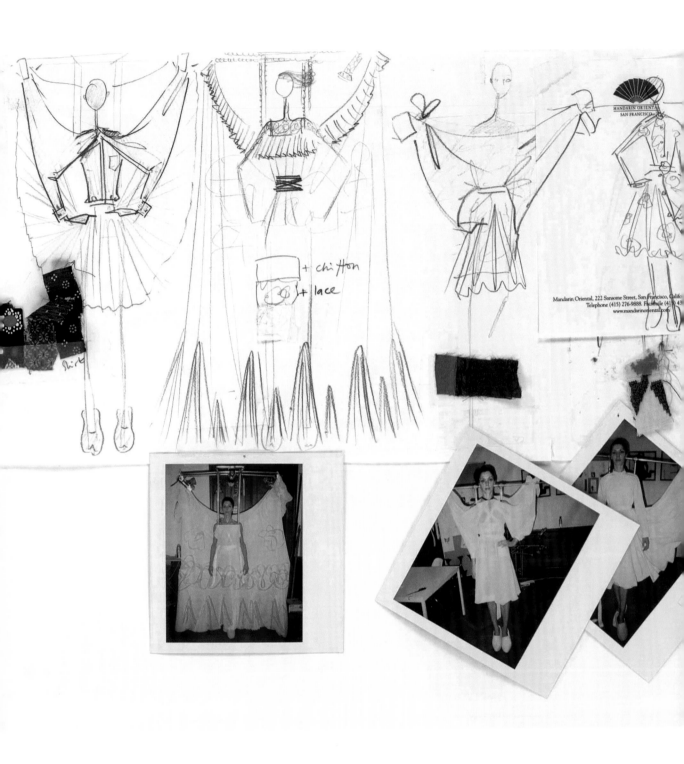

+ chiffon
+ lace

198

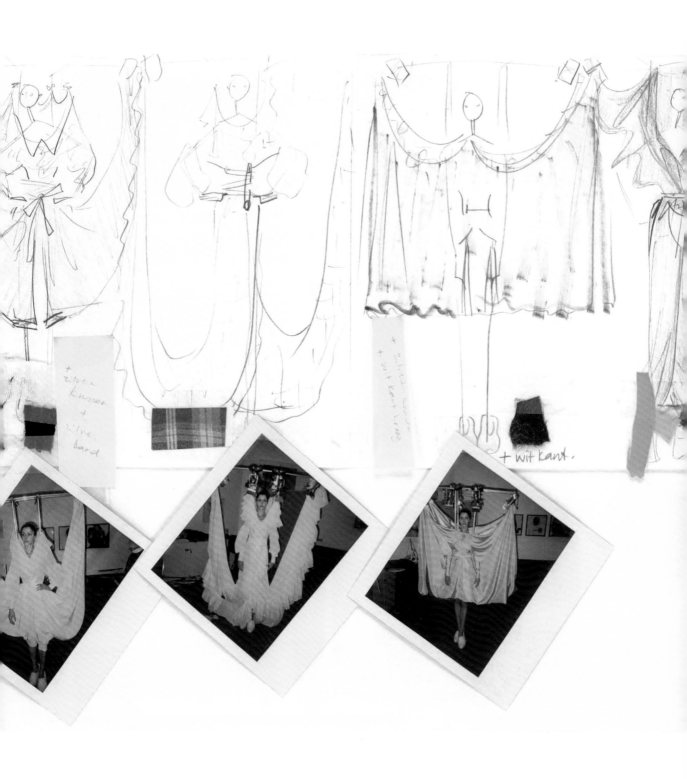

opposite:
'Maryna' doll, 2008

above:
Photograph: Satoshi Saïkusa
Styling: Claudia Englmann
Published in *Vogue Deutsch*, September 2007

Romanticism imbued the 'Harlequin' collection: flowing balloon silhouettes, pompoms, delicate floral patterns and a pastel colour palette were matched with the soundtrack, a mix of Burt Bacharach and Hal David's 'Close to You' of 1970. Any sentiment was offset by surreal touches, especially the familiar use of contrasting scales: models emerged through the wide-open mouth of an enlarged black-and-white photograph of celebrity model Shalom Harlow, taken by long-time Viktor & Rolf collaborators Inez van Lamsweerde and Vinoodh Matadin.

Viktor & Rolf have said that the collection was inspired by the famous French mime artist Marcel Marceau, whom they cite as having cherished everything precious in a cruel world. References were drawn from the *commedia dell'arte*, the inspiration for Marceau's work; from Pierrot, the sad, lovelorn clown in a loose white costume and large pleated collar; and from his counterpart, Harlequin, a Viktor & Rolf staple. Violin motifs, a wink to Man Ray's Surrealist photograph *Ingres's Violin* (1924), appeared throughout the collection, notably the full-size mock violins adorning the last look, a saccharine-pink full-length coat with trademark oversized ruffle.

opposite:
'Magdalena' doll, 2008

Photograph: Paolo Pellegrin
Published in *New York Look*,
January 2008

NO
AUTUMN/WINTER 2008–09

Although often presented as purely conceptual designers, Viktor & Rolf have said that their shows are self-portraits, that they are always an expression of their own state of mind, whether that is one of turmoil or calm, optimism or pessimism. The personal frustration with the fashion industry that gave rise to 'Viktor & Rolf on strike' in 1996 re-emerged in their collection for Autumn/Winter 2008–09. Frustrated here by the relentless turnaround of collections and the inherent commercialism that drives fashion, the designers said in a live interview after the show: 'We love fashion, but it's going so fast. We wanted to say "No" this season' (style.com). 'NO', 'DREAM ON' and 'WOW' were variously sheared, embroidered and scrawled across not only the grey, black and scarlet garments but also the models' faces. In stapling clothes together, a feature of the collection, Viktor & Rolf have said they felt liberated. The staples became a new kind of embroidery.

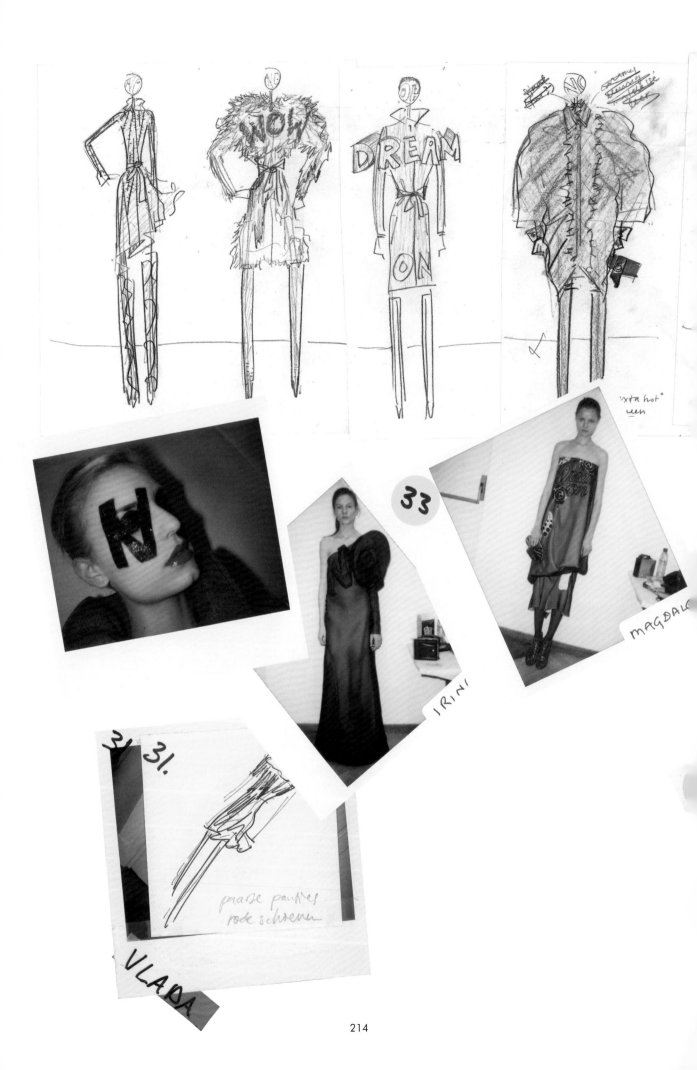

Viktor & Rolf's ascent to fashion superstardom has been an impeccably executed one. Realizing early in their career that a brand is as much about image as about product, the duo placed themselves in the limelight and began commissioning portraits and circulating them in the media. Their image has been compared to that of the art world's most famous duo, Gilbert & George, who likewise are frequently seen together, coordinating their appearance and speaking as one. The effect is twofold: on one level, twins or doppelgängers are immediately arresting visually and look extraordinary; on another, we are encouraged through this image to see Viktor & Rolf as a single creative entity rather than two separate designers working together.

While remaining highly controlled and polished, the duo's image has always retained a knowing, tongue-in-cheek quality that mirrors their ambivalent approach to fashion. It was therefore only natural that, when it came to launching their menswear line, 'Monsieur', in 2003, the designers modelled the clothes themselves, moving and posing in perfect unison like clones. The previous year, a full-page advertisement appeared in the *International Herald Tribune* in which L'Oréal announced its newly forged partnership with Viktor & Rolf. The ad featured a posed photograph of the designers in matching spectacles and outfits, carrying the handwritten message 'Because we're worth it!' While Viktor & Rolf adopted the cosmetic giant's adage, L'Oréal in turn seemed drawn to Viktor & Rolf's strong image.

The numerous portraits of Viktor & Rolf taken over the years are as much a part of their creative output as are fashion or art, and many of these images have been created by two duos who have collaborated with Viktor & Rolf for many years: Inez van Lamsweerde and Vinoodh Matadin, and Anuschka Blommers and Niels Schumm. Others were taken by a variety of high-profile creatives, from the internationally acclaimed Dutch artist Rineke Dijkstra to such established fashion photographers as David Bailey, Kate Barry, Wendelien Daan, Lisa Eisner, Annie Leibovitz, Jean-Baptiste Mondino, Viviane Sassen, Tyen and even fashion guru Karl Lagerfeld.

opposite:
Photograph: Anuschka Blommers and Niels Schumm
Styling: Viktor & Rolf
Published in *Dazed & Confused*, no. 100, April 2003

above:
Photograph: Anuschka Blommers and Niels Schumm
Styling: Viktor & Rolf
Published in *WWD The Magazine*, no. 4, Autumn/Winter 2001–02

Photograph: Lisa Eisner
Styling: Viktor & Rolf
Published in *New York Times Magazine*, 8 December 2002

Photograph: Perou
Published in *Magazine Deluxe*, February 2006

Photograph: Paolo Verzone
Published in *D, la Repubblica delle donne*, August 2006

Photograph: Inez van Lamsweerde and Vinoodh Matadin
Fashion editor: Michel Botbol
Published in *Harper's Bazaar*, May 2000

above, left:
From March 1994 collection
Photograph: Wendelien Daan
Concept: Viktor & Rolf
Published in *Purple Prose*, no. 7, Autumn 1994

above, right:
Michelle, 1995
Jacket from October 1995 collection
Photograph: Inez van Lamsweerde and Vinoodh Matadin
Styling: Viktor & Rolf. Hair: Danillo. Make-up: James Kaliardos
Published in *The Face*, no. 83, October 1995

CHRONOLOGY

Viktor Horsting (b. 27 May 1969, Geldrop) and **Rolf Snoeren** (b. 19 December 1969, Dongen) were born and raised in The Netherlands. They met when they both applied to the Arnhem Academy of Art and Design, where they studied from 1989 to 1992, and began working together upon graduation. In December 1992 they moved to Paris and began producing their own designs.

1993

COLLECTIONS
WOMEN'S
April: Salon Européen des Jeunes Stylistes, Festival International de Mode et de Photographie, Hyères, France (see pp. 40–43)

AWARDS
April: awarded three first prizes at the Salon Européen des Jeunes Stylistes: Prix de la Presse, Prix du Jury, Grand Prix de la Ville de Hyères

1994

COLLECTIONS
WOMEN'S
March: fifteen variations on a white dress (referred to as 'experiments'), incorporating empire lines and puffed ball gowns, as well as amorphous and deconstructed dresses

EXHIBITIONS
February–March: *L'Hiver de l'Amour*, Musée d'Art Moderne de la Ville de Paris, and P.S.1, New York, group exhibition curated by Elein Fleiss, Dominique Gonzalez-Foerster, Bernard Joisten, Jean-Luc Vilmouth and Olivier Zahm, and including Gonzalez-Foerster, Joisten and Vilmouth (see pp. 44–45)
March: *Le Cri néerlandais*, Institut Néerlandais, Paris, group exhibition with Saskia van Drimmelen, Pascale Gatzen, Lucas Ossendrijver and Marel Verheijen

1995

April: move to Amsterdam

COLLECTIONS
WOMEN'S
October: inspired by early twentieth-century Modernist art; included 'Black Square Dress', referencing Kasimir Malevich's painting *Black Square* (1915)

EXHIBITIONS
October: *L'Apparence du Vide*, Galerie Patricia Dorfmann, Paris (see pp. 46–49)
December–January 1996: *Collections*, Galerie Analix, Geneva, group exhibition including Bernadette Corporation and Wolfgang Tillmans

Devon, 1998
Tunic from *Le Regard noir*, 1997
Photograph: Inez van Lamsweerde
and Vinoodh Matadin
Styling: Nancy Rohde

1996

COLLECTIONS
WOMEN'S
March: Viktor & Rolf on strike, Autumn/Winter 1996–97 (see pp. 50–51)
Autumn: a colour palette of white, grey and black; included garments featuring
the strong silhouette of a 1980s torso applied to a light, silk fabric, as well as a
grey bodysuit and a supple white dress

EXHIBITIONS
October: *Launch*, Torch Gallery, Amsterdam (see pp. 52–55)

1997

EXHIBITIONS
April–May: *Viktor & Rolf: Le Regard noir*, Stedelijk Museum Bureau Amsterdam,
with photographs by Anuschka Blommers and Niels Schumm

1998

COLLECTIONS
WOMEN'S
January: first couture collection, défilé haute couture, Spring/Summer 1998
(see pp. 56–63)
July: Atomic Bomb, défilé haute couture, Autumn/Winter 1998–99 (see
pp. 64–77)

Photograph: Anuschka
Blommers and Niels Schumm
Styling: Viktor & Rolf
Published in *Vogue España*,
August 2003

EXHIBITIONS
July–September: *The First 25*, Colette, Paris, group exhibition celebrating twenty-five issues of the magazine *Visioniare*

1999

COLLECTIONS
WOMEN'S
January: Black Light, défilé haute couture, Spring/Summer 1999 (see pp. 78–87)
July: Russian Doll, défilé haute couture, Autumn/Winter 1999–2000 (see pp. 88–97)

EXHIBITIONS
April–May: *Viktor & Rolf: 21st Century Boys*, Aeroplastics Contemporary, Brussels
April–June: *Visions of the Body: Fashion or Invisible Corset*, The Kyoto Costume Institute, and Museum of Contemporary Art, Tokyo, group exhibition including Chanel, Comme de Garçons, Prada and Yves Saint Laurent
May: *Viktor & Rolf*, Visionaire Gallery, New York
May–June: *Creative Time in the Anchorage: Exposing Meaning in Fashion Through Presentation*, Brooklyn Bridge Anchorage, New York, group exhibition with Hussein Chalayan, Susan Cianciolo, Martin Margiela and Vivienne Westwood
June–October: *Heaven: An Exhibition That Will Break Your Heart*, Kunsthalle Düsseldorf, Germany, and tour, group exhibition including Inez van Lamsweerde and Vinoodh Matadin and Thierry Mugler

2000

March: Viktor & Rolf launch their logo, bearing the monogram V&R, based on a wax seal

COLLECTIONS
WOMEN'S
March: Stars & Stripes, first ready-to-wear collection, Autumn/Winter 2000–01 (see pp. 98–101)
July: Bells, défilé haute couture, Autumn/Winter 2000–01 (see pp. 102–11)
October: There's no Business like Show Business, ready-to-wear, Spring/Summer 2001. Outfits based on American sportswear as well as a play on masculine and feminine tailoring. Silver sparkle tape was used for piping and detail. Presented in a musical performance, the clothes were modelled by dancers adopting Busby Berkeley-like formations. Viktor & Rolf joined for a final tap routine

EXHIBITIONS
November–March 2001: *Viktor & Rolf Haute Couture*, Groninger Museum, Groningen, The Netherlands

2001

COLLECTIONS
WOMEN'S
March: Black Hole, ready-to-wear, Autumn/Winter 2001–02 (see pp. 112–19)
October: White, ready-to-wear, Spring/Summer 2002 (see pp. 120–25)

EXHIBITIONS
March–May: *Mohri Color and Space Part 5 [Sayoko]*, Kobe Fashion Museum, Japan, group exhibition including Balenciaga, Chanel, Dior and Jean Paul Gaultier
September–November: YOKOHAMA 2001: International Triennale of Contemporary Art, Japan. An installation titled *The Fashion Designer's Dearest Muse*, consisting of a projection of the 'Black Hole' catwalk show and five large colour photographs by Anuschka Blommers and Niels Schumm featuring sculptural pieces made from press coverage about the collection. Alluding to the fleeting nature of PR, the photographs were reminiscent of seventeenth-century Dutch *vanitas* and still-life paintings. Newspaper editorials were folded using origami techniques, a nod to the Japanese context in which the project was shown

2002

COLLECTIONS
WOMEN'S
March: Long Live the Immaterial (Bluescreen), ready-to-wear, Autumn/Winter 2002–03 (see pp. 126–31)
October: Flowers, ready-to-wear, Spring/Summer 2003 (see pp. 132–41)

AWARDS
October: Fashion and Design Honorees, Fashion Group International's 19th Annual Night of the Stars, New York, dedicated to 'The Provocateurs: Those Who Dare'

opposite:
There's no Business like Show Business, Spring/Summer 2001

above:
Suit from There's no Business like Show Business, Spring/Summer 2001
Photograph: Inez van Lamsweerde and Vinoodh Matadin
Fashion editor: Melanie Ward
Published in *Harper's Bazaar*, March 2001

From *The Fashion Designer's Dearest Muse*, YOKOHAMA 2001: International Triennale
of Contemporary Art, Japan, September–November 2001
Photographs: Anuschka Blommers and Niels Schumm

2003

COLLECTIONS
WOMEN'S
March: One Woman Show, ready-to-wear, Autumn/Winter 2003–04 (see pp. 142–49)
October: The Red Shoes, ready-to-wear, Spring/Summer 2004 (see pp. 150–53)

MEN'S
January: 'Monsieur', Autumn/Winter 2003–04. Menswear line launched, modelled entirely by Viktor & Rolf mirroring each other from opposite ends of the stage and complemented by a male voice repeating the name 'Viktor & Rolf' in a variety of languages, like a mantra. The line answered the designers' need for clothes that they could not find anywhere else: classic but with a dash of humour and informality
June: 'Monsieur', Spring/Summer 2004

MENS- AND WOMENSWEAR
September: capsule collection, Autumn/Winter 2003–04, for La Redoute. Viktor & Rolf designed a selection for men and for women based on such updated classics as the smoking jacket, the white shirt and the shirt dress

EXHIBITIONS
October–January 2004: *Viktor & Rolf par Viktor & Rolf, première décennie*, Musée de la Mode et du Textile, Paris. Highlights from the first ten years of Viktor & Rolf's work, subtitled 'the first decade' rather than a retrospective. Opened with wax figures of the designers. The idea of a zoo was used for the display: garments were shown in glass 'cages', beside which miniature screens featured the respective catwalk shows, with running subtitles describing the garments, as though the clothes were captured in their natural habitat

'Monsieur', Autumn/Winter 2003–04

2004

COLLECTIONS
WOMEN'S
March: The Hunt, ready-to-wear, Autumn/Winter 2004–05
October: Flowerbomb, ready-to-wear, Spring/Summer 2005 (see pp. 154–63)

MEN'S
January: 'Monsieur', Autumn/Winter 2004–05
June: 'Monsieur', Spring/Summer 2005

AWARDS
January: *Elle* Sweden Style Awards, International Designers of the Year, Stockholm
September: Stelle della Moda, Avant-garde Designers, San Remo, Italy; Dutch *Elle* Style Awards, International Designers of the Year, Amsterdam

EXHIBITIONS
April–December: curators of and participants in *Fashion in Colors: Viktor & Rolf & KCI*, The Kyoto Costume Institute, and Mori Art Museum, Tokyo
May–August: *Goddess*, ModeMuseum, Antwerp, Belgium, group exhibition
June–September: *Skin Tight: The Sensibility of the Flesh*, Museum of Contemporary Art, Chicago, group exhibition with Hussein Chalayan, Martin Margiela and Walter Van Beirendonck
September–January 2005: *Spectres: When Fashion Turns Back*, ModeMuseum, Antwerp, Belgium, and tour to Victoria and Albert Museum, London, group exhibition with Hussein Chalayan, Shelley Fox and Christian Lacroix
September–January 2005: *Fashination*, Moderna Museet, Stockholm, group exhibition with Vanessa Beecroft, Alexander McQueen and Martin Margiela

The Hunt, Autumn/Winter 2004–05

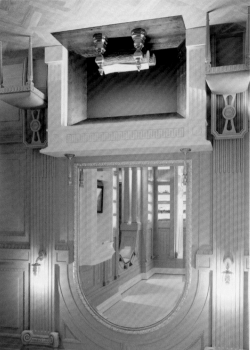

FRAGRANCES
October: launch of first fragrance for women, Flowerbomb, L'Oréal's first collaboration with a fashion designer since Giorgio Armani, seventeen years earlier. The designers invented the name, created the fragrance and were given complete freedom to design and develop the packaging and bottle

THEATRE
November: costumes for dance production by Robert Wilson and Nederlands Dans Theater III, *2 Lips and Dancers and Space: A Dance in Four Parts*

2005

April: first Viktor & Rolf boutique opens on Milan's Via Sant'Andrea, designed by Siebe Tettero. Based on a classic French boutique, the opulent Neo-classical interior is completely unique in a signature Viktor & Rolf way: all the furniture and fittings hang upside down

COLLECTIONS
WOMEN'S
March: Bedtime Story, ready-to-wear, Autumn/Winter 2005–06 (see pp. 164–71)
July: Precollection, Spring 2006
October: Upside Down, ready-to-wear, Spring/Summer 2006 (see pp. 172–77)

MEN'S
January: 'Monsieur', Autumn/Winter 2005–06
June: 'Monsieur', Spring/Summer 2006

AWARDS
June: La Kore, Oscar della Moda, Taormina, Italy
October: *Telva* magazine, International Designers of the Year, Madrid

Viktor & Rolf boutique, Milan, 2005

EXHIBITIONS
September–December: *Dutch at the Edge of Design: Fashion and Textiles from The Netherlands*, The Museum at FIT, New York, group exhibition with Gijs Bakker, Hella Jongerius, Job Smeets and Marcel Wanders

2006

COLLECTIONS
WOMEN'S
January: Precollection, Autumn 2006
March: Silver, ready-to-wear, Autumn/Winter 2006–07 (see pp. 178–87)
July: Precollection, Spring 2007
October: Ballroom, ready-to-wear, Spring/Summer 2007 (see pp. 188–95)

MEN'S
January: 'Monsieur', Autumn/Winter 2006–07
June: 'Monsieur', Spring/Summer 2007

MENS- AND WOMENSWEAR
November: Viktor & Rolf ♡ H&M. Described by the designers as a short love affair between two unlikely partners, H&M and Viktor & Rolf, resulting in a marriage complete with wedding dress – the antithesis of a high-street garment. The men's clothes featured arrow motifs, while the women's carried love hearts

AWARDS
May: Scottish Fashion Awards, International Designer of the Year

EXHIBITIONS
July–October: exhibition design for *Women from Tokyo & Paris*, Van Gogh Museum, Amsterdam, and performance, *La Femme française, la femme japonaise*, with music by Eddy De Clercq

Publicity image for Viktor & Rolf ♡ H&M, 2006
Photograph: Inez van Lamsweerde and Vinoodh Matadin

November–March 2007: *Skin + Bones: Parallel Practices in Fashion and Architecture*, The Museum of Contemporary Art, Los Angeles, and tour, group exhibition including Hussein Chalayan, Comme des Garçons, Frank Gehry, Herzog & de Meuron and OMA/Rem Koolhaas

November–March 2007: *Fashion Show: Paris Collections 2006*, Museum of Fine Arts, Boston, group exhibition including Karl Lagerfeld for Chanel, John Galliano for Christian Dior, Christian Lacroix and Maison Martin Margiela

FRAGRANCES

October: launch of first fragrance for men, Antidote, as finale of the 'Ballroom' catwalk show

2007

COLLECTIONS
WOMEN'S

January: Precollection, Autumn 2007

February: The Fashion Show, ready-to-wear, Autumn/Winter 2007–08 (see pp. 196–203)

June: Precollection, Spring 2008

October: Harlequin, ready-to-wear, Spring/Summer 2008 (see pp. 204–11)

MEN'S

January: 'Monsieur', Autumn/Winter 2007–08

June: 'Monsieur', Spring/Summer 2008

AWARDS

October: *Marie Claire*/Fragrance Foundation Grand Prix du Parfum, Meilleur Parfum Masculin (Best Masculine Perfume) for Antidote

EXHIBITIONS

May–September: *Picture House*, Belsay Hall, Northumberland, England, group exhibition including Mike Figgis, Antony Hegarty and Tilda Swinton

2008

COLLECTIONS
WOMEN'S

January: Precollection, Autumn 2008

February: No, ready-to-wear, Autumn/Winter 2008–09 (see pp. 212–17)

June: Precollection, Spring 2009

MEN'S

January: 'Monsieur', Autumn 2008

June: 'Monsieur', Spring 2009

Antidote publicity still, 2006
Photograph: Inez van Lamsweerde and Vinoodh Matadin

HYÈRES (pp. 40–43)
1993

Grey wool jersey evening gown machine embroidered with silver sequins; grey wool and black polyester bolero

Collection Centraal Museum, Utrecht, The Netherlands (purchased with the support of the Mondriaan Foundation 2000)

L'HIVER DE L'AMOUR (pp. 44–45)
1994

Three white PVC and satin day gowns

Collection Centraal Museum, Utrecht, The Netherlands (purchased with the support of the Mondriaan Foundation 1998)

L'APPARENCE DU VIDE (pp. 46–49)
1995

Gold coated polyester tunics and trousers; black silk organza 'shadows'

From top: Galliera, Musée de la Mode de la Ville de Paris; Viktor & Rolf Archives, Amsterdam; Collection Centraal Museum, Utrecht, The Netherlands (purchased with the support of the Mondriaan Foundation 1998)

VIKTOR & ROLF ON STRIKE (pp. 50–51)
Autumn/Winter 1996–97

Black-and-white print on paper
Dimensions: 44 × 62 cm (17¼ × 24½ in.)

Collection Rob van de Ven and Corinne Groot, Amsterdam

LAUNCH (pp. 52–55)
Torch Gallery, Amsterdam, 1996

'Catwalk': MDF catwalk, plastic doll, stroboscope

Viktor & Rolf Archives, Amsterdam

'Design Studio': MDF and metal drawing table, drawings, toiles, patterns, hangers

Collection Rob van de Ven and Corinne Groot, Amsterdam

'Boutique': metal clothes rail, hangers, clothes, glass

Witzenhausen Gallery, Amsterdam

'Photo Shoot': plastic doll, paper, Polaroids

Witzenhausen Gallery, Amsterdam

'Perfume Stand': MDF stand, glass and MDF display cabinet, lightbox, perfume bottles

Viktor & Rolf Archives, Amsterdam

FIRST COUTURE COLLECTION
(pp. 56–63)
Spring/Summer 1998

'Porcelain'
White silk organza day gown; unglazed bisque porcelain hat and necklace

Collection Groninger Museum, Groningen, The Netherlands

'No'
White silk gazar trouser suit with black silk gazar ruffle detailing

Collection Groninger Museum, Groningen, The Netherlands

ATOMIC BOMB (pp. 64–77)
Autumn/Winter 1998–99

'Harlequin'
Cuir de coton trouser suit with cushions

Collection Groninger Museum, Groningen, The Netherlands

RUSSIAN DOLL (pp. 88–97)
Autumn/Winter 1999–2000

Collection Groninger Museum, Groningen, The Netherlands

'First preparation'
Nude silk satin and coarsely woven natural jute dress

'Balloons'
Black silk organza dress; pink, red, green, yellow and blue silk 'balloons'; white silk satin ribbon

Collection Groninger Museum, Groningen, The Netherlands

'Second preparation'
Cream cotton lace and natural jute dress with Swarovski crystals and bead embroidery

'Tuxedo'
Black wool crêpe trouser suit with silk satin detailing; white silk crêpe georgette shirt with cushions

Collection Groninger Museum, Groningen, The Netherlands

'Third preparation'
Natural jute dress with gold-brown Swarovski crystals

BLACK LIGHT (pp. 78–87)
Spring/Summer 1999

'Hate'
Black silk gazar tailcoat and trousers; white silk gazar ruffle shirt

Collection Groninger Museum, Groningen, The Netherlands

'Fourth and fifth preparations'
Natural jute dress and vest with multicoloured Swarovski crystals

'Friend'
Black silk gazar evening dress with white silk gazar asymmetrical sleeve

Viktor & Rolf Archives, Amsterdam

'Sixth preparation'
Yarn printed silk taffeta dress; natural jute vest with multicoloured Swarovski crystals

'Seventh preparation'
Natural jute and printed lurex lace coat; multicoloured Swarovski crystal bracelets

'Eighth preparation'
Natural jute coat with multicoloured Swarovski crystals

'Final preparation'
Natural jute grand cape and corsage

STARS & STRIPES (pp. 98–101)
Autumn/Winter 2000–01

'Full ensemble'
Red-and-blue screen print on white cotton coat, trousers, skirt, ruffle shirt and ankle boots

Collection Groninger Museum, Groningen, The Netherlands

BELLS (pp. 102–11)
Autumn/Winter 2000–01

'WWWXXX "Dawn" Would You Like Another Transaction? World Wide Web Pornography'
Dark green heavy twill cotton coat with silver- and gold-coloured brass bells; light green silk crêpe georgette evening gown

Collection Groninger Museum, Groningen, The Netherlands

'CIA DMZ "WASP" YOU'VE GOT MAIL Central Intelligence Agency Demilitarized Zone'
Black silk organza evening gown with silver- and gold-coloured brass bells

Collection Groninger Museum, Groningen, The Netherlands

BLACK HOLE (pp. 112–19)
Autumn/Winter 2001–02

'Devon'
Black wool and polyester lurex evening ensemble

Collection Groninger Museum, Groningen, The Netherlands

'Mini'
Black fox-fur jacket with black silk ribbon closure; black silk crêpe georgette dress with silk satin tape detailing

Collection Centraal Museum, Utrecht, The Netherlands

WHITE (pp. 120–25)
Spring/Summer 2002

'Madelaine'
White silk organza five-layered bow shirt; white silk crêpe georgette trousers with silk satin detailing

Collection Groninger Museum, Groningen, The Netherlands

'Zuzana'
White silk organza shirt and trousers

Collection Groninger Museum, Groningen, The Netherlands

Wedding dress of Her Royal Highness Princess Mabel van Oranje-Nassau, 2004
Dove-white double-faced duchesse satin dress; white silk grand georgette bows and ribbons; white silk tulle veil

Courtesy Her Royal Highness Princess Mabel van Oranje-Nassau

LONG LIVE THE IMMATERIAL
(BLUESCREEN) (pp. 126–31)
Autumn/Winter 2002–03

'Karolina'
Chromakey blue cotton shirt with cotton
and silk military detailing; wool trousers
with wool and silk military detailing;
blue leather boots

Collection Centraal Museum, Utrecht,
The Netherlands

'Rasa'
Black wool and silk satin trouser suit;
grosgrain lurex ribbons and bows;
plastic helmet

Collection Centraal Museum, Utrecht,
The Netherlands (purchased with the support
of the Mondriaan Foundation 2005)

FLOWERS (pp. 132–41)
Spring/Summer 2003

'Erin'
Black heavy cotton twill coat with
black and multicoloured silk flowers
and sequinned lining

The Kyoto Costume Institute, Japan

'Raquel'
Pink silk chiffon evening dress
with corsage

Viktor & Rolf Archives, Amsterdam

ONE WOMAN SHOW (pp. 142–49)
Autumn/Winter 2003–04

'Simone'
Dark brown wool trouser suit; light
pink, beige and white layered silk
shirts of various textures

The Kyoto Costume Institute, Japan

'Karolina'
Fuchsia, gold, pink and pale pink silk
corsage dress made from various
sized ribbons

The Kyoto Costume Institute, Japan

THE RED SHOES (pp. 150–53)
Spring/Summer 2004

'Mariacarla'
Pale pink silk chiffon dress with
incorporated grey wool trouser leg

Viktor & Rolf Archives, Amsterdam

BEDTIME STORY (pp. 164–71)
Autumn/Winter 2005–06

'Tiiu'
White silk tulle and double-faced
silk ball gown with red silk chiffon,
seed beading and red Swarovski
crystal embroidery

Viktor & Rolf Archives, Amsterdam

'Raquel'
Nude silk tulle evening gown with
incorporated black viscose crêpe
trouser leg

Viktor & Rolf Archives, Amsterdam

'Hana'
Red-and-white silk satin quilted
coat; white and pale pink silk satin
cushions with silk lace and chiffon
appliqué

Collection Centraal Museum, Utrecht,
The Netherlands (loan from H+F Collection 2006)

FLOWERBOMB (pp. 154–63)
Spring/Summer 2005

'Sena'
Black silk satin chiffon and black
polyester satin evening gown; satin
ribbon collar; plastic helmet

Viktor & Rolf Archives, Amsterdam

'Raquel'
Nude silk chiffon evening gown
with silk lace slip dress; bodice
covered with cream silk chiffon
ruffle pillow; red silk satin rose

Viktor & Rolf Archives, Amsterdam

UPSIDE DOWN (pp. 172–77)
Spring/Summer 2006

'Carmen'
Pale gold silk lurex organza shirt;
pale gold silk organza skirt

Viktor & Rolf Archives, Amsterdam

'Mateja'
Pale gold silk lurex organza and silk
organza evening gown fastened with
large golden safety pins

Viktor & Rolf Archives, Amsterdam

SILVER (pp. 178–87)
Autumn/Winter 2006–07

'Solange'
Cotton trench coat with silver-plated
white cotton cuffs; face net of braided
hair

Viktor & Rolf Archives, Amsterdam

'Fabiana'
Blue cotton-silk changeant cocktail
dress with partly silver-plated bodice
and skirt, and silver-plated bow
detailing at waist; silver-plated metal
face net; ruffle silver-plated collier
de chien necklace

Collection Centraal Museum, Utrecht,
The Netherlands (loan from H+F Collection 2006)

'Caroline'
Silver-plated cotton wedding dress
comprising bodice and skirt; silver-
plated metal face net; silver-plated
silk flower bouquet with ribbon
detailing

Viktor & Rolf Archives, Amsterdam

BALLROOM (pp. 188–95)
Spring/Summer 2007

'Caroline'
Nude Lycra tulle, white poplin,
black polyester and wool catsuit
with black silk bow tie

Viktor & Rolf Archives, Amsterdam

THE FASHION SHOW (pp. 196–203)
Autumn/Winter 2007–08

'Emina'
Charcoal-grey jacquard silk taffeta skirt
with black-and-blue cotton jacquard
ribbon detailing; black printed poplin
shirt with checked taping on collar; metal
trusses with incorporated lights and
sound; high-heeled wooden clogs with
hand-painted Staphorst-style pattern

Zuiderzee Museum, Enkhuizen, The Netherlands
Acquisition with financial support of the Mondriaan
Foundation, Amsterdam

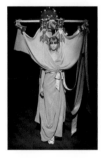

'Raquel'
Orange-, white- and blue-checked
silk georgette chiffon evening gown
with silver clasp closure; metal trusses
with incorporated lights and sound;
high-heeled wooden clogs with hand-
painted Delft blue pattern

Zuiderzee Museum, Enkhuizen, The Netherlands
Acquisition with financial support of the
Mondriaan Foundation, Amsterdam

'Maryna'
Pale blue washed silk evening gown
with burgundy and pale pink silk
satin ribbon sash; metal trusses
with incorporated lights and sound;
high-heeled wooden clogs with
hand-painted Delft blue pattern

Collection Centraal Museum, Utrecht,
The Netherlands (loan from H+F Collection 2008)

HARLEQUIN (pp. 204–11)
Spring/Summer 2008

'Magdalena'
Pink double-faced silk organza
coat; pale pink chiffon dress;
white silk organza cabbage-rose
corsage; fuchsia silk satin violin
corsages with black embroidery
detailing

Viktor & Rolf Archives, Amsterdam

NO (pp. 212–17)
Autumn/Winter 2008–09

'Magdalena'
Grey melange wool coat with
gold-coloured brass 'staples'

Viktor & Rolf Archives, Amsterdam

THE MAKING OF
THE DOLLS

The centerpiece of *The House of Viktor & Rolf* exhibition at the Barbican Art Gallery is a 6-metre-high (19 ft 8 in.) doll's house. Populating the house are some fifty specially designed dolls, each about 70 centimetres (27½ in.) tall and wearing an exquisite, hand-made perfect replica of a signature Viktor & Rolf piece. The dolls are even made up and have their hair styled to look like the model who first wore the clothes at the catwalk show or photo shoot.

Commissioned from a traditional Belgian dollmaker, these dolls combine elements of two types of nineteenth-century European doll: the bisque porcelain faces of French children's dolls, replete with human hair, and the papier-mâché bodies of German fashion dolls.

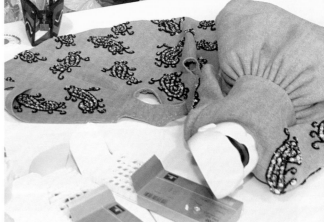

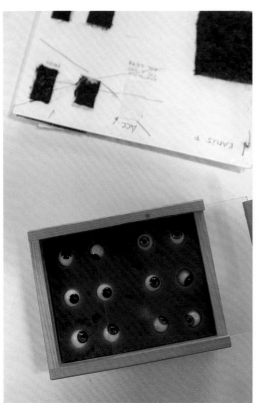

FURTHER READING

Books

MONOGRAPHS

E-Magazine: Viktor & Rolf par Viktor & Rolf, première décennie, exhib. cat., Paris, Musée de la Mode et du Textile, 2003

Fashion in Colors: Viktor & Rolf & KCI, exhib. cat. by Claude Levi-Strauss, Akiko Fukai and Barbara Bloemink, The Kyoto Costume Institute and Tokyo, Mori Art Museum, 2004

Viktor & Rolf, *Viktor & Rolf 1993–1999* (Amsterdam: Artimo Foundation, 1999)

Viktor & Rolf Haute Couture Book, exhib. cat. by Amy Spindler and Didier Grumbach, Groningen, Groninger Museum, 2000

GROUP TITLES

Creative Time in the Anchorage: Exposing Meaning in Fashion Through Presentation, exhib. cat., ed. Patrick Li, New York, Brooklyn Bridge Anchorage/Creative Time, 1999

Caroline Evans, *Fashion at the Edge: Spectacle, Modernity and Deathliness* (New Haven, Conn., and London: Yale University Press, 2003)

———, 'A Monument to Ideas', in *Spectres: When Fashion Turns Back*, exhib. cat. by Judith Clark, Antwerp, ModeMuseum, 2004

Extreme Beauty: The Body Transformed, exhib. cat. by Harold Koda, New York, The Metropolitan Museum of Art, The Costume Institute, 2001

Stephen Gan, *Visionaire's Fashion 2001: Designers of the New Avant-Garde*, ed. Alix Browne (London: Laurence King, 1999)

Picture House: Film, Art and Design at Belsay, exhib. cat. by Judith King, Northumberland, Belsay Hall, 2007

Skin + Bones: Parallel Practices in Fashion and Architecture, exhib. cat. by Brooke Hodge, Patricia Mears and Susan Sidlauskas, Los Angeles, The Museum of Contemporary Art, 2006

YOKOHAMA 2001: International Triennale of Contemporary Art, exhib. cat. by Japan Foundation, Tokyo, 2001

Selected Press Interviews

Román Alonso, 'Double Dutch: The Fantasy Life of That Famous Fashion Duo Viktor & Rolf', *New York Times Magazine* (8 December 2002), pp. 109–15

Elein Fleiss, 'Passive Violent Clothes', *Purple Prose*, no. 7 (Autumn 1994), pp. 70–72

Susannah Frankel, 'v&r', *Dazed & Confused*, no. 87 (March 2002), pp. 130–37

————, 'The Odd Couple: The Wacky World of Viktor & Rolf', *The Independent* (11 November 2006)

Lauren Goldstein, 'Geek Chic', *Time Europe Magazine*, vol. 162, no. 15 (20 October 2003)

Jamie Huckbody, 'The Other Two', *i-D*, no. 197 (May 2000), pp. 100–104

————, 'Because We Want To', *i-D*, no. 235 (September 2003), pp. 197–201

Gert Jonkers, 'Durvenen denken', *Het parool* (9 September 2000), pp. 8–9

Peter de Potter, 'Viktor & Rolf: Hinkstapspringen door modeland', *Weekend knack* (24 February 1999), pp. 270–76

Katja Rahlwes, 'Viktor & Rolf', *Index Magazine*, no. 48 (April 2005)

Pascale Renaux, 'Alter Ego', *Numéro* (July/August 2003), pp. 192–96

Susie Rushton, 'The Odd Couple', *The Independent* (4 October 2003)

Miles Socha, 'Flying Dutchmen', *WWD The Magazine*, no. 4 (Autumn/Winter 2001–02), pp. 96–98

Lucy Stehlik, 'Viktor & Rolf: Fashion Geeks', *icon*, no. 30 (December 2005), pp. 89–94

Polly Vernon, 'We Are One Brain, One Person, One Designer', *The Observer* (13 November 2005)

Selected Articles and Publications

Gina Bellafante, 'This is Paris: No Giggling, Please', *New York Times* (12 March 2001)

Tamsin Blanchard, 'Global Warning', *The Observer Magazine* (21 May 2000), pp. 12–15

Meredith Etherington-Smith, 'Double Dutch', *Sunday Telegraph Magazine* (28 February 1999), pp. 32–35

Bridget Foley, 'Going Dutch', *W* (September 1998), pp. 234–35

Cathy Horyn, 'Two Dutch Designers Take Couture to the Surreal Side', *New York Times* (1 June 1999)

Laurence Hovart, 'Mode portrait: Viktor et Rolf en quête de statut', *Vogue Paris* (December 1998–January 1999)

Alice Jones, 'Inside the Madhouse', *The Independent Extra* (27 June 2007), pp. 12–13 [Belsay Hall exhibition review]

Armand Limnander, 'Double Dutch', British *Vogue* (November 2002), pp. 143–44

Richard Martin, 'Viktor & Rolf: Le Regard noir', newsletter of Stedelijk Museum Bureau Amsterdam (1997)

Suzy Menkes, 'Viktor & Rolf: Concept to Concrete', *International Herald Tribune* (8 October 2003)

William Middleton, 'New Amsterdam', *Harper's Bazaar* (May 2000), pp. 191–94

———, 'Cutting-Edge Classics', *Harper's Bazaar* (October 2003), pp. 218–23

Carol Mongo, 'Viktor & Rolf: Out of This World Fashions', *Paris Voice* (November 2003)

Ian Phillips, '21st Century Boys', *The Independent Magazine* (3 October 1998)

———, 'Head Over Heels: We Flipped for Viktor & Rolf's Upside-Down Milan Store by Tettero and SZI Design', *Interior Design* (June 2005)

Olivier Saillard, 'Viktor & Rolf: Couturiers de l'apparence', *Connaissance des arts* (February 2001), pp. 79–84

James Sherwood, 'Double Dutch', *The Independent Review* (16 January 2003)

Miles Socha, 'Dutch Masters of Couture RTW', *WWD* (2 November 2000), p. 14

André Leon Talley, 'The Flag Bearers', American *Vogue* (May 2000), p. 150

Jonathan Turner, 'Dutch Courage', *Black + White Magazine*, no. 45 (September 2000), pp. 48–50

Evelien van Veen, 'Viktor & Rolf's magiska modecirkus', *Elle* Sweden, no. 3 (Spring 2001)

Viktor & Rolf, 'Collection No. 1: Détachement', *Purple Prose*, no. 4 (Autumn 1993)

——— [contributors], *Visionaire*, no. 26: *Fantasy* (December 1998)

——— [contributors], *Visionaire*, no. 44: *Toys* (November 2004)

——— [contributors], *Visionaire*, no. 48: *Magic* (February 2006)

David Woolf, 'Far-Flung Dutchmen: Viktor & Rolf', *Couture Eve Mode* (1994), pp. 116–17

Olivier Zahm, 'Golden Boys', *Artforum*, vol. 33, no. 4 (December 1995), p. 81

Multimedia

Loud and Clear: Viktor & Rolf + Toek Numan + Saatchi & Saatchi, DVD (Gateshead, BALTIC Centre for Contemporary Art, 2003)

Viktor & Rolf: 'Because We're Worth It!' The Making of a Fashion House, documentary directed by Femke Wolting (2005), distrib. Submarine Channel, The Netherlands

Photograph: Anuschka Blommers and Niels Schumm
Styling: Viktor & Rolf
Published in *Vanity Fair*, February 2003

ACKNOWLEDGEMENTS

Barbican Art Galleries and Viktor & Rolf would like to thank the following for making this publication, exhibition and associated events programme possible:

Patricia Morvan and Anne-Lyse Tardivat, **Agence VU**; M.C.A. Baroness Taets van Amerongen; Alex van der Zouw, **Amitek Prototyping**; Julian Mills Arnold; Phillipe Brutus, Eleanor Oakes and Lindsay Thompson, **Art + Commerce**; Candice Marks, **Art Partner**; Joyce Bastinck, **Beauty Base London**; Paul Sumner, **Benchworks**; Patricia Martinez, **Blanpied Rubini**; Anita Bossinade; Bas Bossinade; Professor Christopher Breward; Elizabeth Kerr, **Camera Press**; Emma-Jane Cammack; Cecile Ogink and Cunera van Rossum, **Centraal Museum, Utrecht, The Netherlands**; Judith Clark; Cristina Palumbo, **Condé Nast Italia**; Shelley Halperin, **Condé Nast Publications**; Andrea Vollmer-Hess, **Condé Nast Verlag**; Bronwyn Cosgrave; Marianne Croes; Oriole Cullen; Patricia Dorfmann; Piet van der Sluis, **Dutch Molds**; Deborah Saron, **Lisa Eisner studio**; Toby Elizabeth Shaw, **Arthur Elgort studio**; Lorraine Candy, Mel Hutcheon and Anna Pursglove, **Elle UK**; Stella di Meo and Daphne Thissen, **Embassy of the Kingdom of The Netherlands**; Freya Elliott and Judith King, **English Heritage Contemporary Art Programme**; William Ling, **Fashion Illustration Gallery**; **Firma Zwartz**; Lyndsay Black and Jameson Walthers, **firstview.com**; Edward Fornieles; Eloise Fornieles; Hadley Freeman; Stephen Sorrell, **FUEL**; Joëlle Chariau, **Galerie Bartsch & Chariau**; Meyken Geertsen; Ton van Leen and Walter van Groningen, **Gerlach Art Packers & Shippers BV**; Chris Gooch; Marten de Leeuw, **Groninger Museum, Groningen, The Netherlands**; Christer Helgesson, **H&M**; **Hans Boodt Mannequins**; **Heinen-Delftware**; Mark McKenna, **Herb Ritts Foundation**; Bernard Terrie and Mia Terrie, **Het Gents Poppenatelier**; Patricia van Heumen; Jos Hogenkamp; William To, **Hong Kong Design Centre**; Cathleen Wolf, **Markus Jans studio**; Sija Jansen; Ton Joling; all at **Karla Otto**; Naomi Kashiwagi; Miho Miyachi, **Katy Baggott Ltd**; Jonny Koppenol; Rie Nii, **The Kyoto Costume Institute, Japan**; Brian Anderson, **Inez van Lamsweerde and Vinoodh Matadin studio**; Rosalinda Laurens; Annabel Lewis; Tanya Ling; all at **L'Oréal**; **Lyppens**; Kirstie Mcleod; Nick Galvin and Billy Macrae, **Magnum Photos**; Daniela Balzarotti, **Management+Artists+Organization**; Margarethe Hubaure, **Margarethe Hubaure – International Illustration**; Penny Martin; Nicola Bailey, Claire Chandler, Michelle Draycott and Hugh Merrell, **Merrell Publishers**; **Mevis & Van Deursen**; Ferry van der Nat; Fans Ottink; Grayson Perry; **Pineapple Dance Studios**; Joyce Postumus;

Sandy Powell; Esther Muñoz and Hester Swaving, **Premsela, Dutch Platform for Design and Fashion**; **Print Unlimited**; Caroline Gaimari, **Purple**; Anna van Lingen, **Rijksmuseum Amsterdam**; Wendy Gallagher, **The Roundhouse**; Marten Loonstra, **Royal Collection, The Hague**; Seamus Ryan; Tomoko Sato; Charlène Limoges, **SEED**; Malin Huber, **David Sims studio**; **Solstiss Lace**; Katie Fash, **Mario Sorrenti studio**; Paul Haworth and Alex Brenchley, **Stedelijk Museum, Amsterdam**; Peter Stigter; Ischa Stuart; Siebe Tettero and Meike Stoetzer, **Tettero**; José Teunissen; Gary Thorne; Ms. Troost; Lou Taylor, **University of Brighton**; Mark Eastment, **Victoria and Albert Museum**; **Videopolis**; Bram Claassen, Martin van Dusseldorp, Jarrod Glaze, Vanja Hedberg, Sophie van der Heijden, Wim de Kanter, Debby Koot, Esther Koster, Min Liu, Elnaz Niknani, Saskia Stockler, Joost van Vollenhoven, Jessica Voorwinde, Hinke van Weperen, Danielle Windsor, and the entire team, **Viktor & Rolf**; **Viva Cake**; **Vleminckx**; Roger Tredre, **World Global Style Network**; Jack Yuan; Diana van Zeil

Lenders to the Exhibition
Centraal Museum, Utrecht, The Netherlands
Galliera, Musée de la Mode de la Ville de Paris
Groninger Museum, Groningen, The Netherlands
Han Nefkens, H+F Collection
The Kyoto Costume Institute, Japan
Her Royal Highness Princess Mabel van Oranje-Nassau
Rob van de Ven and Corinne Groot, Amsterdam
Witzenhausen Gallery, Amsterdam
Zuiderzee Museum, Enkhuizen, The Netherlands

Partners
Mondriaan Foundation, Amsterdam
Premsela, Dutch Platform for Design and Fashion
VandenEnde Foundation

Associate Partners
Arnhem Nijmegen Cool Region
Embassy of The Kingdom of The Netherlands
KLM Royal Dutch Airlines
Made in Arnhem

Media Partner
Elle UK

Further Assistance
Fashion, the Body & Material Cultures Research Centre (University of the Arts London)
Pernod Ricard UK
Swarovski

PICTURE CREDITS

INDEX

THE AUTHORS

Caroline Evans is Professor of Fashion History and Theory at Central Saint Martins College of Art and Design at the University of the Arts London. She has contributed to a number of fashion publications and is the author of *Fashion at the Edge: Spectacle, Modernity and Deathliness* (2003).

Susannah Frankel is Fashion Editor of *The Independent* newspaper and Fashion Features Director of *Another Magazine*.

Official copyright © 2008 Barbican Centre, City of London. The Authors and Artists
Design and layout copyright © 2008 Merrell Publishers Limited

First published 2008 by Merrell Publishers Limited
in association with Barbican Art Gallery on the occasion of the exhibition
The House of Viktor & Rolf, 18 June–21 September 2008

Barbican Art Gallery
Barbican Centre
Silk Street
London EC2Y 8DS

barbican.org.uk

Exhibition Development
Curator: Jane Alison
Assistant Curator: Ariella Yedgar
Exhibition Assistant: Jessica Rolland
Interns: Vanessa Carlos, Tamsin Clark and Miwa Takamura
Exhibition Design: Siebe Tettero
Exhibition Graphic Design: Murray & Sorrell FUEL

Merrell Publishers Limited
81 Southwark Street
London SE1 0HX

merrellpublishers.com

British Library Cataloguing-in-Publication Data:
Evans, Caroline
The House of Viktor & Rolf
1. Viktor & Rolf (Firm) – Exhibitions
I. Title II. Frankel, Susannah III. Barbican Art Gallery
746.9'2'0922

ISBN-13: 978-1-8589-4460-9
ISBN-10: 1-8589-4460-0

Produced by Merrell Publishers Limited
Designed by Murray & Sorrell FUEL
Copy-edited by Philippa Baker
Proof-read by Caroline Ball
Indexed by Ursula Caffrey

Printed and bound in Germany

pages 8–9:
Photograph: Anuschka Blommers
and Niels Schumm
Published in *The Independent Magazine*,
3 October 1998

Front cover photograph: Anuschka
Blommers and Niels Schumm, 2008

Back cover photograph: Inez van
Lamsweerde and Vinoodh Matadin, 2002

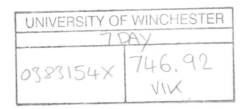